CW00661647

KNOWLEDGE AND THE FUTURE SCHOOL

'This is the book that many secondary school heads of department, frustrated by a focus on the pedagogic 'how?' at the expense of the disciplinary 'what?', have long been wanting their senior leaders to read. The authors' message is bold and its implication clear: disciplinary knowledge and curriculum thinking must become nothing less than the central concern of leadership, the essence of staff development and the driver of whole-school debate.'

CHRISTINE COUNSELL, *Senior Lecturer, Faculty of Education, University of Cambridge, UK*

'You don't need to agree with every argument in this highly engaging book to appreciate the importance of its challenges. Let's think about what schools are actually for. Let's stop seeing their important work only in terms of data, targets, what can be measured. Here are some serious (but far from dull) arguments about knowledge and the work of schools. This book cuts across the usual political debates and point-scoring. It is a model of how to write well for an audience that should include teachers and head teachers, parents, the public – and politicians.'

LYN YATES, *Foundation Professor of Curriculum, University of Melbourne, Australia*

'Knowledge and the Future School is an intelligent and courageous book that takes the reader to the very heart of what a good education in our schools should be. The authors have adeptly argued the case for a subject-led curriculum that not only enlightens, stretches and challenges the pupil but also brings joy in learning and teaching.'

DANA ROSS-WAWRZYNSKI DBE, *CEO and Executive Head Teacher at Bright Futures Educational Trust and Altrincham Grammar School for Girls, UK*

'This book raises important questions about the place of knowledge in education and society. Whether you agree with all the answers or not, any serious minded educator or researcher with an interest in social justice, should pay careful attention to the arguments that Young and his collaborators are making.'

KERI FACER, *Professor of Educational and Social Futures, University of Bristol, UK*

'This will not be an uncontroversial book – certainly not amongst politicians of either left or right. It is an important one, however. For passionate teachers everywhere, drawn into teaching by their love of their subject and the emancipatory power of education, it will be one which re-inspires them to think more deeply about what should be taught in their classrooms. The challenge to teach 'powerful knowledge', which liberates the mind and gives young people the ability to engage critically with the world will resonate deeply with teachers whose intrinsic motivations have always been to educate without dogma. This book's proposed 'Future 3' model will help teachers to transcend the sterility of the current ideological debate and fashion a future for their schools and pupils where deep educational values can take centre stage.'

JON COLES, *Group Chief Executive, United Learning, UK*

'Rather than simply critiquing recent educational reforms, the authors of this book offer school leaders and teachers a clear and practicable way of thinking about knowledge and the curriculum. This way of thinking affirmatively links pupils' entitlement to knowledge with social justice through the development of knowledge-led schools and curricula. After nearly three decades of reform aimed at de-professionalizing educators, this book ultimately makes an urgent and persuasive case for their re-professionalization in the name of providing pupils with more equitable access to powerful knowledge.'

BRIAN D. BARRETT, *Associate Professor,*
Foundations and Social Advocacy Department,
The State University of New York College at Cortland, USA

'I thoroughly recommend this book. It is carefully argued, thought-provoking and timely. Surely we can now move away from the often sterile and simplistic debates, "knowledge versus skills". *Knowledge and the Future School* presents us with a tantalizing alternative that will allow us to embrace the goal of widening access to "powerful knowledge" through teaching framed by subjects, while at the same time celebrating the diverse experiences of students.'

DAME CELIA HOYLES, *Professor of Mathematics Education,*
Institute of Education, University of London, UK

KNOWLEDGE AND THE FUTURE SCHOOL

Curriculum and social justice

MICHAEL YOUNG AND DAVID LAMBERT WITH CAROLYN ROBERTS AND MARTIN ROBERTS

BLOOMSBURY ACADEMIC

LONDON • NEW YORK • OXFORD • NEW DELHI • SYDNEY

BLOOMSBURY ACADEMIC
Bloomsbury Publishing Plc
50 Bedford Square, London, WC1B 3DP, UK
1385 Broadway, New York, NY 10018, USA

BLOOMSBURY, BLOOMSBURY ACADEMIC and the Diana logo
are trademarks of Bloomsbury Publishing Plc
First published 2014
Reprinted by Bloomsbury Academic 2015, 2017, 2018, 2019 (five times)

A catalogue record for this book is available from the British Library.

Young, Michael F. D.
Knowledge and the future school : curriculum and social justice / Michael Young
and David Lambert ; with Carolyn Roberts and Martin Roberts.
pages cm
ISBN 978-1-4725-3473-6 (hardback) – ISBN 978-1-4725-2814-8 (paperback)
1. Education–Curricula–Great Britain. I. Lambert, David, 1976- II. Title.
LB1564.G7Y68 2014
375'.001–dc23
2014003620

ISBN: HB: 978-1-4725-3473-6
PB: 978-1-4725-2814-8
ePDF: 978-1-4725-2954-1
ePub: 978-1-4725-3454-5

Typeset by Newgen Knowledge Works (P) Ltd., Chennai, India
Printed and bound in Great Britain

To find out more about our authors and books visit
www.bloomsbury.com and sign up for our newsletters.

CONTENTS

FOREWORD

The timing of any publication is important. Knowledge and the Future School is no exception. It appears at the end of a 'long decade' in which an increasing number of educators began to express concerns about the 'retreat from knowledge' in schools and classrooms. Initially, these arguments generated a good deal of reaction, since they seemed to call for a return to an 'imagined past' and to evoke the unhappy educational politics of the 1980s where a series of governments seemed to want to revive a 'curriculum of the dead' (of course, this debate is alive and well in the light of the current Secretary of State for Education's pronouncements on the content of school subjects). Although there were some reservations, many 'progressive' educators accepted the modernizing thrust of New Labour's education policies in which schools were places where the dead hand of tradition was to be replaced by a modernized form of school knowledge where learning mattered more than teaching, and developing 'new kinds of smart' was to be encouraged. This was to be supported by the architecture of school improvement, overseen by a committed cadre of school leaders equipped with the types of knowledge-building capacities found in go-ahead corporations. In this brave new educational world, the 'what' of curriculum seemed less important than the 'how' of learning.

This narrative was interrupted by the economic crash of 2007–8, and subsequent concerns about inequality and social injustice. Put simply, what do ever-improving examination results mean if they do not result in social mobility? In this context, the question of 'what schools are for', and, more specifically, what concepts and content are to be learned in schools, is beginning to be posed more frequently and with greater urgency. Knowledge and the Future School is, to my mind, the strongest and most important exploration of these issues to date, and one that deserves the widest possible reading.

The book's importance is heightened (and given dramatic force) by the fact that its principal author, Michael Young, was one of the prominent figures when, four decades ago, an established curriculum orthodoxy was in the process of being overturned. At that time, the postwar project of educational expansion for all children was widely seen to have failed, and writers associated with the so-called new sociology of education argued that a key element in the disaffection and failure of many children was a curriculum based on elite and middle-class world-views and values. What was required, they argued, was a revision of curricula and school subjects that would better reflect the experiences and backgrounds of 'ordinary kids'. It is important to realize that this became professional orthodoxy over the following two decades: knowledge was a social construction and, as such, the subjects represented an 'arbitrary' collection of facts and concepts. Crucially, the arguments about school knowledge were framed in terms of social justice. A curriculum that was relevant to the interests and concerns of excluded groups could increase participation and motivation in schooling.

In Knowledge and the Future School, the authors explain why they no longer subscribe to this earlier position, and, more than that, set out to explore the implications for practice in schools. However, the argument they make here retains a strong focus on the notion of social justice. Having access to knowledge is still important, but the terms have been reversed: it is access to the 'powerful knowledge' found in school subjects that offers the best option for ensuring access to the things that all should expect in a 'good society' (decent work, housing and culture). While Young's changed perspective is often interpreted as a personal volte face (and indeed that is one element of the story told in this book), I think it is better to understand it as a continuing engagement with the question of social democracy: what both the 'early' and 'late' Young share is a central engagement with the question of how to ensure that all children (irrespective of social characteristics of class, gender and ethnicity) have access to knowledge. This is the promise of education and is a project that has defined (and continues to shape) the work of schools and teachers. This becomes clear in the second part of this book with its powerful discussions of what it means to live within current educational orthodoxies. Thus in Martin Robert's account of his time as a headteacher we get a moving account of the tightening grip of an 'anti-knowledge' educational ideology, while Carolyn Roberts describes a putative account of what an alternative might be for schools. These are brave contributions, not least because they attempt to speak in a different language and register to the dominant techno-speak of school leadership paradigms.

The authors of this book realize that their position in relation to 'knowledge' may be misinterpreted by some as a call for a narrow and limiting curriculum in schools. Such misinterpretations reflect the dominance of both the 'constructivist' view – which sees knowledge as malleable and transitory – and an instrumentalism that focuses more on the outputs of education (expressed in examination results) than the content of the curriculum. To counter this, the authors anticipate and answer a number of stock concerns that have been raised by headteachers and teachers. They call for an open and honest debate.

For me, the wider significance of this book is the extent to which it can be read as a cultural critique of British society. The extent to which schools and teachers seem to have given up on knowledge is a reflection of how society has given up on ideas of Enlightenment and modernity. The fact that this is happening in schools clearly shocks and dismays the authors. Of course, readers may contest this portrayal of the state of schooling. The immediate question that Knowledge and the Future School prompts is whether there are collective forces and voices that can challenge the current position. This remains an open question, but the challenge for headteachers to take a role in intellectual leadership is one that may appeal.

Finally, although the book is clearly rooted in a British (perhaps even English) context, this in no way diminishes the relevance of the arguments for other national education systems. Over the past three decades education in advanced economies has been recalibrated as a tool for the production of 'human capital' suited for life in a 'knowledge economy'. This book dares us all to create different educational imaginaries.

John Morgan

Auckland

November 2013

PREFACE

Why should you read this book?

You are a busy member of a busy school leadership group. At the end of another day it occurs to you that, as well as your life being measured out in coffee spoons, it appears to be dominated by tables, graphs and charts. You look back over the day, the month, the year since the last results and wonder how many more times before the next set you might need to go through the achievement data with colleagues, governors, scrutineers and yourself. You note that you spend so much time with the data registrar that you might as well move her into your office and have done with the pretence that you actually do anything else. Sorting out truculent adolescent behaviour is a blessed relief some days: at least it puts a face to another name on the lists and lets you solve something for yourself.

As you wait for the internet to turn its attention to your data needs you ponder the nature of education and its relationship to your current role. You think wistfully, if not entirely accurately, about your years as a head of department and the pleasure you found in your subject. You do not miss it all, but you do miss the conversation with colleagues about the values of that particular novel or field trip or experiment. Occasionally you wonder what children are meant to make of our obsession with achievement and assessment rather than the *stuff* they are learning.

A young person loiters vaguely by your door. His mum wants him to check his targets again, so you go over his last report for the third time. He seems satisfied with your explanation and conveys himself back to maths. When you asked him if he enjoyed maths he said he was doing better this term than last and is on target for a C, a relief to you both. But in your darker moments you wonder what he actually knows, what will remain in his head after the next exam and what he will have made of his education once he moves on. Will he know enough to make a success of life? What knowledge, you ponder, will help him to understand and make sense of the world? Does he know enough of science, poetry and human endeavour to encourage and sustain him? What have you actually done for him other than measure his 'attainment'.

We have written this book primarily for those thousands of teachers, many in senior positions, others at an early stage of their career, who have such dark moments. It is also written for governors too and educationists who are presently wondering whether the time innumerable school leaders are spending on their school data is actually time *well spent*. While this may help them improve their position on the local league tables and their Ofsted grades, is it really in the interests of their pupils? Furthermore, for school leaders who want to nourish and cherish new entrants to the profession who are often fired by a passionate desire to make a difference: is the obsession with data and performance management really in the interests of releasing the talents of our best teachers?

Our argument is that what matters most is the curriculum – what pupils actually learn which will help them have successful and fulfilling lives. We want our colleagues to engage now in serious debate about what young people should know and understand in this day and age; about what constitutes genuine knowledge and understanding; about the significance of established subjects to all pupils; and about by whom and how the curriculum and its constituent elements should be defined and updated.

You should read this book since Michael Young here explains his concept of 'powerful knowledge' and its potential for transforming the way in which we think about the curriculum for all pupils. Young's writings have strongly influenced our thinking about knowledge and about subjects and why they are important to all pupils. He argues persuasively that in a democratic society which prizes equality of opportunity the curriculum should be based first and foremost on the knowledge we consider all young people should have access to and begin to acquire during their school years.

We outline in this book a progressive, subject-based approach to curriculum thinking which should lie at the very centre of school leadership. We also make the case for the urgent reprofessionalization of teachers so government can shift to them and our university colleagues' greater responsibility for the school curriculum, its assessment and its development.

The past few years have seen a plethora of government educational initiatives which have created a sense of near-chaos in education policy making in England. In the world of education this is a time of great unease therefore, with government and teachers at loggerheads. We explain how we have got to this uncertain state and suggest a way forward.

We know that you do not have much leisure for such philosophizing, but we think that you should. We offer you these thoughts so that you can make your school a better place.

Carolyn Roberts and Martin Roberts

ACKNOWLEDGEMENTS

The editors would like to thank John Morgan (University of Auckland) for his helpful comments on the earlier chapters and Camilla Erskine for unfailing support, encouragement and wise advice throughout the writing of this book. We would also like to thank Professor Elizabeth Rata for giving us permission to include a revised version of a paper that originally appeared in the *Pacific Asian Education Consortium Journal* as Chapter 4 of this book.

NOTES ON CONTRIBUTORS

David Lambert was a secondary school geography teacher for 12 years becoming a Deputy Headteacher in 1985. He joined the Institute of Education (IoE) in 1986–7 as a teacher educator, becoming Reader in Education in 1999 and Assistant Dean ITE (research). He played a leading role in introducing the innovative Master of Teaching (MTeach) course at the Institute which now has over 200 students. In 2002, he left the IoE to become full-time Chief Executive of the Geographical Association, now a significant provider of CPD and a leader in funded curriculum development activity. From September 2007–12, he combined this role with a return to the IoE as Professor of Geography Education (returning full time to the IoE in 2012). He leads the online MA Geography in Education (www.mageoged.webs.com). Recent publications include *Geography 11–19: A Conceptual Approach*, co-written with John Morgan (2010), and *Debates in Geography Education*, co-edited with Mark Jones (2013).

Carolyn Roberts read theology at university and taught in schools in London, the Midlands and the North East. She was formerly Head of St Hild's Church of England School in Hartlepool and then of Durham Johnston School, a comprehensive school nationally recognized for high levels of progression from its sixth form to the most competitive universities and courses. She is currently Head at Thomas Tallis, a large 11–18 comprehensive school in Greenwich.

Martin Roberts studied History at university and taught in schools in Leeds, Essex and Bedfordshire before becoming Headteacher of the Cherwell School, Oxford, a coeducational 13–18 comprehensive school. While he was there Cherwell almost doubled in size and emerged as a leading local school. Since 2002 he has been a member of the Steering Committee of the Prince's Teaching Institute, now a major national provider of subject-centred CPD. An author of numerous textbooks, he has also written the histories of two Oxford schools.

Michael Young is part-time Professor of Education at the Institute of Education, University of London, UK. He studied natural sciences and, later, sociology at university, and taught chemistry for five years in a London secondary school before joining the IoE as lecturer in sociology of education. He later became Head of the Post 16 Education Centre. Throughout his career his main research and teaching have been concerned with questions about knowledge, curriculum and qualifications. His publications include *Knowledge and Control* (1971), *The Curriculum of the Future* (1998), *Bringing Knowledge Back In* (2008) and *Implementing National Qualifications across Five Continents*, co-written with Stephanie Allais, (2013). Several of these books have been translated into other languages. His forthcoming book is *Knowledge, Expertise, and the Professions* (Routledge, 2014), co-edited with Johan Muller.

Introduction

Michael Young, David Lambert,
Carolyn Roberts and Martin Roberts

We are writing this book at a time of enormous uncertainty about the implications of the new government policies, and much anxiety about the future for those working in schools and in teacher education. These anxieties arise partly from the policy of economic austerity and its overall effect on public spending. Despite the government's commitment to 'ring-fencing' the schools budget, the broader decision to reduce public expenditure wherever possible is beginning to be felt by individual schools; for example, through the cuts in the educational maintenance grants and other welfare benefits which impinge indirectly on schools with a significant proportion of pupils from low-income families. Under such pressures, schools have less time and spare resources for innovation and thinking through how to respond to the new policies.

The government's new emphasis on academic subjects (symbolized by the EBacc[1]) poses quite new questions for heads and their teachers,

---

[1] EBacc refers to the English Baccalaureate introduced by the government to recognize all students with Grades A*–C in English, Mathematics, a Science, a Foreign Language and a Humanities subject.

which are independent of whether they are sympathetic to the reforms. Another pressure on teachers and heads which has a longer history is the far greater focus on student examination grades, not just as evidence of rising levels of pupil achievement but as a basis for improving their school's position on the league tables. No less important has been the need for a school to be rated 'outstanding' or at least 'good' by Ofsted.[2] The emphasis on testing and grades impacts equally on students for whom 'getting a higher grade' can take over any intrinsic interest they might have in the subjects they are studying, and as a result reduce their commitment and motivation for learning and, potentially, the quality of their work.[3] A third factor is the speed of the government's reforms since 2010 and the extent to which they challenge much that schools had got used to in the previous decade. These challenges arise not only from the reform of the National Curriculum and examinations at 16+, but from the increased pressure for schools to apply for 'academy' status, and the new responsibilities that this involves. With such a range of changes happening at the same time, it becomes increasingly difficult for headteachers to take advantage of the greater autonomy that the government intends its reforms to give them. In practical terms, headteachers and their colleagues may easily feel that they have less autonomy not more, especially in relation to the curriculum. This is the difficult context in which we argue that the curriculum and

---

[2]The official body for inspecting schools in England.

[3]The issue of what has become known as 'teaching to the test' and the extent to which it is a response to external pressures, deserves much more attention than we can give it in this book. The more tests and examinations are used as measures of accountability and not primarily as evidence of what pupils have learned, the more teachers will be drawn to focus on tests as ends not means.

curriculum leadership by headteachers becomes a more, not less, important issue for schools.

The aim of this book

The aim of this book is not to prescribe what schools should do in the new circumstances or to propose yet another new curriculum. It aims to be a resource for headteachers and their staff in *thinking about* the curriculum. We start from the assumption that in the new context that schools face, heads and their senior staff are going to have to give more emphasis to being curriculum leaders as well as managers of staff, pupils and finances, important though these responsibilities are. Secondly, curriculum leadership involves not just making practical decisions to ensure a school's survival; it requires a set of curriculum priorities that define the purposes of the school and each of its departments.

Too little emphasized, in current debates, is that as members of the teaching profession, heads and their teachers, and others working in education, have specialist knowledge about education; they are, in other words, a society's educational experts – in a similar way that social workers, doctors and lawyers are experts in their fields. It is this expertise which is the basis of their autonomy and the trust that parents have in them. It also gives them the knowledge, and the responsibility to reflect on the current reforms and their implications and think about what alternatives their school may offer their students. This is not to deny that in certain ways, teachers are in a more difficult position than other professions; there is a sense in which everyone thinks they 'know about education' in ways which they do not about the law or their health. However, the reality is, as with all professions, that parents and governments have to trust teachers and schools – they are not in schools and classrooms as teachers are. The question for both schools and governments is how they respond to their different responsibilities. When only a small proportion of those attending school were expected to show any evidence of what they had learned, trust was not a problem. Selecting out the majority of pupils at 11, or later at 14 or 15, meant those who stayed on were, almost by definition 'high achievers' and questions of trust and standards hardly arose. Today the situation is very different. As increasing numbers stay on at school for longer we expect much more from our schools without considering enough whether we as a society provide our teachers with the resources they need. This issue is beyond the scope of this book. However, as the PISA (Program for International Student Assessment) tables show, there are surely lessons to be learned from 'high-trust' systems such as Finland and Germany. The former is 'successful' with the vast majority of each cohort without any form of external inspection, whereas in Germany, one of the highest measures of school standards, the Abitur examination (a broader equivalent of English A levels) is entirely assessed by teachers in individual schools.

This book aims to be a contribution to supporting the teaching profession in fulfilling society's trust in them. A more confident sense of their own expertise is surely the best basis for the teaching profession as a whole to take advantage of the greater responsibilities that schools now have. The clearer sense a school has of its purposes, the stronger will be the trust in it held by parents and the better position it will be in to deal constructively with external demands, such as their positioning on league tables or changing Ofsted guidelines. If there is one factor that stands out in the countries with the most successful systems of public education, it is the trust that such countries place in their teachers.

Ourselves and our potential readers

The rationale for writing this book now is that, whatever one's views about the current government's reforms and their practicality, they challenge some most deeply felt current assumptions about education, what it is to be a teacher and the links between education and equality. While many in the educational community have reacted negatively to the reforms, there is no doubt that they offer us a once in a generation opportunity to discuss and debate what we want our schools to do.

In coming together to write this book, we formed an unusual, and for us a highly productive team. We include a former RE teacher and experienced headteacher who has recently taken on the headship of a large comprehensive school in south London (Carolyn Roberts); a former history teacher and comprehensive school head, and now adviser to the Prince's Teaching Institute (Martin Roberts); a teacher educator and former Chief Executive of the Geographical Association (David Lambert); and a former science teacher and now sociologist of education who specializes in curriculum theory (Michael Young). Our collaboration on this book has not been just a question of two 'practitioners' coming together with two 'theorists'; Carolyn and Martin are widely read and informed about current 'educational theory' and its many strengths and weaknesses. The need that we felt to write this book arose from coming to similar conclusions from strikingly different starting points and experiences. If anything, it was the 'practitioners' who convinced the 'theorists' that writing the book was worthwhile.

Bringing together our very different experiences has led us to ask questions that we have found most current educational research does not ask. We do not expect you to always agree with us and we do not apologize for being controversial, and maybe upsetting some readers. However, we hope that the book will stimulate debate among the staff of schools and that the kind of questions we ask will help you to think in new ways about what your school is doing for your pupils, and how you may be able to do it differently, and hopefully, better.

Those who we hope will be our readers can be divided into the following groups:

- heads, senior teachers and classroom teachers (largely but not solely those in secondary schools);

- student teachers and those doing masters degrees and research in education, and teacher educators. For this particular group, at the end of the book, we provide a list of books and papers which takes further some of the issues we raise;

- government officials and their advisers, members of governing bodies, employers, and local authority staff. We hope they will benefit from the insights the book offers into how policies impact (both positively and negatively) on the day-to-day working of schools;

- parents with children at school who we hope the book will encourage to participate in discussions about the future of the school their child is attending – and lastly;

- the students themselves: 'consumers' as they are sometimes referred to. We reject the latter term, for you cannot buy or consume knowledge.

We hope that the book will also be read by the 'regulators' – the exam boards, Ofqual and Ofsted. Examination boards and Ofqual play a significant role in interpreting the National Curriculum and defining the knowledge content of school subjects and how they are related to university-based disciplines. As David Lambert explains in Chapter 7, these bodies have in effect replaced the more organic links between school subject teachers and specialists in the disciplines based in the universities.[4] We hope that this book will help examiners and inspectors clarify their assumptions about what schools can and cannot do and remember that it is the *curriculum*, as a statement of the purposes of a school, that should lead examining and inspection, and not, as is too often the case, the reverse.

Finally, we have our international audience in mind as educational issues become increasingly global. We hope that the ideas will resonate with you despite your very different experiences of education. Much of what Michael Young and David Lambert have learned about education is as a result of visiting other countries and having discussions with teachers and teacher educators and

---

[4]It is interesting and from the point of view of this book, welcome, that the present government is proposing a stronger role for the universities in the development of A level syllabuses and forms of assessment.

researchers. The lens of comparison gives us a unique mirror to see the weaknesses of our own system and even sometimes, its strengths.

However, it is the senior staff in schools that we have most urgently in mind in writing this book. In complex and difficult circumstances, they face most directly the implications of current reforms. For them and the teachers who work with them, we hope the book offers a helpful framework for thinking about the decisions that they have to make. The decisions we have in mind range widely; they not only include the selection of staff, finance, timetabling and deciding what courses to offer, but they also include the professional judgements involved when teachers ask pupils to undertake activities in individual lessons and for homework. The question 'what educational purpose does it serve?' applies as much to the big whole school decisions about staffing and the timetable as it does to a teacher deciding to 'correct' or 'challenge' a pupil's assignment or response in class. The book aims to be a resource for thinking and for sharing our thoughts and ideas with those who have to make difficult educational decisions at every point of their professional lives.

1

Knowledge, curriculum and the future school

Michael Young

This book focuses on the curriculum; however, as we hope is already clear, it is not a curriculum handbook. It aims to offer a way of thinking about the curriculum. In this chapter, we use the term 'curriculum' as a kind of short hand for defining *the purpose of a school* (or, in relation to the National Curriculum, the aims of the school system of a country), whether from the perspective of a head, a subject leader, a teacher, a parent or pupil, or a minister. In focusing on the curriculum and not on the more immediate questions of inspections, staffing finance, league tables or pupil behaviour, we do not dismiss such issues but emphasize *ends* rather than *means*. In other words, we ask how such managerial issues might be best understood from the point of view of a school's curriculum purposes. We try to ask questions that point to alternative solutions and we hope that they offer you a more strategic basis for dealing with the immediate problems with which you are faced.

We do not set out to be primarily critics of government policies or to endorse them; the educational and national press is full enough

of both. In a sense we want to stand back a bit from the warring
factions that dominate today's educational debates. The issues in
these debates are deeply felt on both sides; however they do not do
the profession, or the government much good, especially in the eyes
of parents. In contrast we go back to first principles and a view about
what we see as the main purpose of schools. Our experiences suggest
that these purposes, although rarely articulated, are more widely
shared by teachers and parents than is often assumed. The main
purpose of schools can, we argue, be summarized as follows:

> It is to enable all students to *acquire knowledge* that takes *them
> beyond their experience*. It is knowledge which many will not have
> access to at home, among their friends, or in the communities in
> which they live. As such, access to this knowledge is the 'right' of
> all pupils as future citizens.

Such a definition needs more elaboration that relates to our view of
knowledge than there is space for here. The importance of subjects
is crucial and is discussed in some detail in Chapters 4 and 7.

Being clear about the purposes of schools will, we believe, help
heads and their staff to think beyond the immediate issues that the
new policies and even the perennial problems present them with.

Schools, especially secondary schools with their range of subject
specialists, have more autonomy than often they are themselves
aware of. The professional experience of teachers tells them what
it is that schools can do and what they cannot. Political pressures
from governments of all political parties often expect schools to
solve problems that have their origins elsewhere and which schools
alone can never solve – especially through the curriculum. Typical

examples are teenage pregnancy, obesity, youth unemployment or an assumed lack of civic responsibility among teenage boys and girls. Developing specific curriculum responses to such problems is, we are sure, a mistake. This is not to play down their importance, but to suggest that they are more likely to be solved from a clear understanding of their causes, rather than by assuming that they are problems that can be dealt with 'educationally'. For example; youth unemployment is largely caused by a lack of demand for youth labour; more employment-related curricula will not change such a lack of demand. This is not, of course to say that the kind of approach to the curriculum that we advocate will not, by strengthening the intellectual resources of young people by the time they leave school, play a role in enhancing their employment prospects and better prepare them for the responsibilities they will face as adults.

The more heads and teachers are clear about the main purpose of schools, the less vulnerable they will feel when faced with attempts to use the curriculum as a solution to problems that schools will never themselves be able to solve.

The question of knowledge

Our view of the primary purpose of schools takes us directly to the question of knowledge – as the *entitlement of all pupils* – and to the question, 'OK, but what knowledge?' That is why Carolyn Roberts (Chapter 6) and David Lambert (Chapter 7) refer to the idea of the 'knowledge-led school'. It is also why any strategy for promoting social justice and greater educational equality has to begin with the question of 'knowledge'.

Paradoxically, knowledge is an uncomfortable word for many in education today. It is sometimes seen as the special concern of philosophers and best avoided by the rest of us, or it is associated with a top-down Gradgrind version of teaching that becomes little more than the mechanical 'transmission of facts' from teacher to pupils. For some teachers, knowledge has elitist and exclusive connotations; it is negatively associated with elite fee-paying schools and is assumed to involve imposing something on many pupils against their will and without any respect for the knowledge and experience that they bring to school. The Brazilian Adult Educator Paulo Freire expressed this view most evocatively as a 'banking model' of education, or as he put it 'depositing' knowledge in the 'empty heads' of learners. Although Freire was writing about the education of poor adults in rural communities in Chile and not about schools, his 'banking' model captured the imagination of many idealistic teachers from the 1970s, especially those working with inadequate resources in schools located in disadvantaged communities. It seemed to describe what they found themselves doing and not what they had hoped to do in deciding to become teachers. *Pedagogy of the Oppressed*, the title of his justly famous book, not only sold more than a million copies but also inspired many, in schools as well as in adult education. It offered the hope, however lacking in detail, that somehow a different kind of education was possible that involved a genuine dialogue with pupils and would really serve their interests, however disadvantaged their circumstances. I was a young lecturer when Freire's book was first published in the 1970s, and it certainly inspired me and many involved in teacher education at the time. We wanted our student teachers to be able to do something different immediately and thought Freire was telling us what it was. It was no fault of his that his idea of 'conscientization' led to a one-sided emphasis on 'practice' and experience; the result, of course, was that the link between knowledge and practice got lost. It is the idea that access to knowledge beyond our experience is the only true source of freedom and as such is the 'entitlement of all' that underlies this book. For some this idea will be as difficult and even as alien as it was once for me. The title of my first book was *Knowledge and Control* (1971) and it criticized the curriculum in terms similar to how Freire's ideas were interpreted. It took me a long time to recognize that freedom from the existing curriculum without access to knowledge leads nowhere.

The school, for all its tendencies to reproduce the inequalities of an unequal society, is the only institution we have that can, at least in principle, provide every student with access to knowledge. The only alternative to schools for all is to accept that the majority will never have the educational opportunities that the minority has always treated as their right. We must respect and value the experience of pupils, but we can never allow them to depend on their experience alone. To do so would leave them (and us) in the position of our Stone Age ancestors, or worse; we would be no different from animals, who have *only* their experience.

For those readers who disagree with this argument about the importance of knowledge, I can only ask you to trust us and read on and make your own judgements when you come to the end.

We do not deny the persuasiveness of the ideas of those who see knowledge as a form of domination, nor do we dismiss the integrity of many of those adopting such ideas; they are an understandable response to the disaffection of many pupils and the endless imposition of new policies from governments of all parties. On the other hand, we think that such a negative view of knowledge is deeply mistaken and lies at the heart of the sense of disillusionment shared by many who work in education today. Real educational change will always be slow because the learning involved in acquiring real knowledge takes time and can challenge the deepest identity of learners. Freeing pupils from the limitations of their experience, which is what schools at their best can do, is always potentially 'alienating';[1] however just to leave students with their experience as something almost untouchable will only perpetuate current inequalities. You can be absolutely certain that the rich and powerful will always make sure that their children are not left with just their experience – you only have to look at the curriculum of a typical Public School – it never focuses on their pupils' experience!

Knowledge is not only uncomfortable for many teachers, but it is also a tricky word in the English language; it has so many meanings. For example, we refer to our local 'knowledge' when we list the names of the streets we live but we also refer to our 'knowledge' (or lack of knowledge!) about quantum theory. In this book we start with view that as educators, we must differentiate *types of knowledge*: in particular between the knowledge that pupils bring to school and the knowledge that the curriculum gives them access to. This view does not involve any esoteric philosophical distinctions, nor will it be wholly unfamiliar to readers of this book. Despite this it is all too often dismissed by educationalists. It is a distinction that is related to the experience familiar to many who, like I did, opted for

---

[1] It separates a person from their prior and often deeply embedded sense of themselves.

teaching as a career with the expectation that they would be able to inspire the next generation to be scientists, historians, geographers or poets – in my case it was chemists! This is a view of knowledge as worthwhile in itself because it is in some sense the truest knowledge we have about the world and therefore must be transmitted to the next generation.

The approach to knowledge we take in this book is different from this view in two respects. First, those graduates who became (and many who still do become) teachers, like I did, took the knowledge they had acquired at university for granted, as largely given, and relatively static. They had what in Chapter 2 we will refer to as Future 1 view of knowledge. To put it another way, a Future 1 view assumes that though the future will be different from the past, it will always be an extension of the present. Secondly, whatever their politics, few of those teachers envisaged how the knowledge they wanted to 'pass on' could or even should be an entitlement 'for all'; they accepted that it was knowledge 'for some'. In this they were following a distinguished tradition of 'liberal education' associated with such writers as Matthew Arnold and Cardinal Newman in the nineteenth century and leading later in the twentieth century to I. A. Richards, F. R. Leavis and T. S. Eliot among others.

So what is the idea of knowledge that we want to share with you in this book, and why is acquiring it seen as so problematic and divisive that teachers often avoid the question of knowledge altogether? The most important starting point for us is to recognize that all knowledge is inescapably a human product that is developed by people in every period of history and in every society to make sense of the world they experience. At the same time, knowledge is progressive; in very different ways in different fields from the sciences to the humanities, it changes and develops. Our knowledge is different from, and in some senses and in some fields, better than the knowledge of previous generations. Secondly, as a human product, knowledge is, in principle, accessible *to all human beings*, even if we construct ideas and concepts such as 'measurable intelligence' that makes this seem all but impossible for the majority. Children have very different experiences after they are born which shape their development, but we have no reason or evidence that leads us to believe that, except for a tiny minority with the most acute learning difficulties, they can be differentiated at birth in their capacities to acquire the foundations of knowledge. This differentiation of capacities begins in the early years; but as we know from the research, much is a product of differing circumstances. A third feature of our view of knowledge is that in the past two centuries, the ways that new knowledge has been discovered have become increasingly specialized. As a consequence, not all can be research scientists or lawyers or novelists or engineers; no one can know everything. Specialization is double-edged; it has brought with it all the benefits associated with modern societies and at the same time it has led to new divisions and new inequalities. This is a tension that all modern societies have to acknowledge and come to terms with. However, in a book primarily concerned with the idea that everyone is entitled to a *foundation* of knowledge, we have no space to consider the conditions for or consequences of specialization in the later years of schooling. We recognize that, to a different extent in different countries, many will not acquire the foundations of knowledge by the same age; some will progress faster while others will need extra support over a longer period if they are to progress. Countries vary significantly in whether their priority is ensuring that as large a proportion of each cohort as possible progresses together, and those which accept the inevitability of differentiation and hence, inequalities from an early age.

Finally, an important aspect of our view of knowledge that is crucial in any discussion of the curriculum is that it is distinguished from opinions or common sense. Unlike common sense it is *never* something 'given' and never tied to specific contexts. It is always fallible and open to question, in principle, by anyone, although the more specialized the knowledge, the harder it will be for non-specialists to question. It is its fallibility that tells us that however true something is it is only the truth *as far as we know*. For example, for 2,000 years, mathematicians thought that Euclid's axiom that 'parallel lines never meet' was true. Since Lobachevsky and others, in the nineteenth century, we now know that Euclid's axiom is only true in certain circumstances. It is this openness that distinguishes knowledge in the sense used in this book from our everyday experience and lies at the root of its links with freedom; it always opens up new possibilities. The extent to which these new possibilities are open to those who have not followed a specialist route of study varies widely across different fields. The fallibility of knowledge also distinguishes it from the knowledge associated with dogma or ideology which always rely on some overt or covert force to resist any challenge. It is the fallibility of knowledge, its openness to question and the alternatives that it points to that provide the most powerful argument against the 'fear of knowledge' often found among teachers. Knowledge, from the perspective we are presenting, is always about possibilities – it is the antithesis of fear.

A last point: we need knowledge to live in a complex world but we cannot live by knowledge – we live by beliefs in what we value which may or may not be the beliefs of a religion. What is important is not, as Richard Dawkins and others claim, that religion is a delusion. Although religious ideas are not knowledge in the sense we use the word in this book, they are one of the sets of values which people live by; as educators we must respect such beliefs and values even when we do not share them.

Pedagogy and the acquisition of knowledge

There is another neglected or, more appropriately, misunderstood feature of knowledge that is important for our argument in this book. Unlike gaining a new experience, acquiring what in Chapter 3 we will refer to as 'powerful knowledge', always requires much dedicated effort and hard work. Experience is just experience – what we are. Knowledge, like anything worthwhile, is not only shared but has to be struggled for – wrought from the world by work no less dedicated than the work it took to create it. Students are not always convinced of this argument and they find support in much advertising and mass media which presents a world in which everything is made simple and accessible to anyone (provided you have the money!). The argument of this book and, less explicitly, all public demands for higher educational standards, is that schools and teachers have to help students go beyond and sometimes resist the cultural forces that they experience everyday. It is not surprising that some students, when they find something difficult to understand, assume it is not worth struggling with. All too easily, they become satisfied with 'passing' or accept the label that they are 'non-academic' or 'slow learners'. The concept of a 'slow learner' is always preferable; whereas slow learners can always learn more, the label 'non-academic' creates an identity which may be hard to change.

It is the sense of the struggle involved in acquiring knowledge that may be at the root of the prevailing 'fear of knowledge' found among teachers. The idea of 'encouraging students to learn' seems much gentler and more democratic. On the other hand, it can easily lead a teacher to forget to ask the more difficult questions such as 'what are they learning?' and 'is it valuable?' This is a genuine problem facing teachers and we will return to it later in the book. It is why the term pedagogy, which describes the professional practice of teachers, is so important but so often undervalued. For us pedagogy refers to the theory and practice involved in taking students beyond their experience and helping them to acquire new knowledge.

We should not be surprised that making new knowledge one's own is difficult and some students will always resist it or try to avoid the difficulty by 'memorizing' and regurgitating it. Not only is knowledge the product of many people's hard and dedicated work in the past, but real knowledge challenges not only what we know but sometimes our sense of who we are. It was not just that Pope Urban disagreed with Galileo about the sun going round the earth; he felt as if his whole being as head of the Church was under threat. Breaking with our sense of who we are is never easy – another reason for a far greater acknowledgement of the enormous responsibility we place on teachers.

Learning at school – from experience to knowledge

We have schools, colleges and universities which provide students with opportunities to break with their past experience and begin to trust the possibilities that knowledge and a *knowledge-based* curriculum can offer them. With its combination of reliability and fallibility, what we refer to as 'powerful' knowledge has little to do with the piling up and regurgitating of facts that an emphasis on knowledge is all too easily associated with. This does not mean there is knowledge without facts, just that facts *on their own* are not knowledge. Knowledge in the sense we are using the word in this book allows those with access to it to question it and the authority on which it is based and gain the sense of freedom and excitement that it can offer.

There are some parallels as well as important differences between acquiring knowledge and tough manual tasks like digging ditches or cutting logs. Such 'hard work' was paid work until we developed machines for digging and cutting much faster than men and women ever could. We now have machines not only for doing hard manual work like digging ditches, but computing machines for doing hard mental work like solving complicated mathematical problems which would take a person, however skilled, half a life time or more. When we argue that the acquisition of knowledge is always 'hard work', we mean something very different from the hard work either of digging or of the repetitive routines of computers. It is the 'hard work' of making a relationship with ideas that are new to the learner. The school curriculum and the pedagogy of teachers can offer pupils ways of relating to knowledge that is new to them and new in how this knowledge relates to their experience. Whether pupils acquire this new relationship between knowledge and their experience is largely the responsibility of teachers and the confidence they have in their subject and their pedagogy. Another way of grasping the meaning of the term pedagogy refers to the *relationship between teachers and pupils* that are involved in development of their knowledge. It is why technology, however sophisticated it is and despite its many remarkable capacities for making information accessible, will never replace teachers or schools – acquiring knowledge involves a human relationship with teachers who are specialists in pedagogy. This does not deny that parents and peers may not at times take on the role of teacher in the same sense that they may take on the role of healer. The important difference is that teachers are involved in pedagogy as specialists and schools are specialist institutions that bring teachers and students together.

Curriculum and social justice

The subtitle of this book is Curriculum and Social Justice – not words that are commonly found together in writing about education.[2] Why is this so when the links might at first glance appear obvious? No one thinks of separating medical knowledge (the basis, in a sense of the 'hospital curriculum') from health

---

[2]The journal of Education Policy recently had a special issue on the theme 'What would a socially just education system look like?' With one exception, a short comment by the Australian sociologist Raewyn Connell which we refer to later in this book, there is virtually no reference to the curriculum or knowledge at all.

rights and justice. There are two possible reasons which take us to the heart of our argument in this book. The first arises from the reality that we have a system in which systematic educational inequalities persist. If we take a broad definition of 'entitlement to foundation knowledge' to be 5 good (C grade or better) GCSE's in the EBacc subjects, this currently includes significantly less than half of secondary school pupils in English schools[3] – a clear expression of educational inequality. Furthermore in their emphasis on 'standards' measured by performance in more rigorous examinations, the present curriculum and examination reforms seem likely to exaggerate this inequality. It is for this reason that many working in education oppose the reforms, but without proposing any alternative approach to tackling existing inequalities. Those who criticize the government reforms appear to accept, or at least prefer the situation that existed under the previous government when the links between curriculum and standards were, at least partially obscured. First, pass rates rose every year for over 30 years and this made a debate about whether standards were rising or not seem irrelevant. Secondly, and less explicitly, the idea of 'universal' standards for all was dropped in 2007 when different ways of measuring achievement for different subjects and forms of assessment were treated as 'equal'. The assumption was that giving priority to a list of *more difficult* 'academic' subjects put children of wealthier parents at an advantage, either because they could pay for private schooling or additional tutoring or because they provided other out of school cultural advantages.

---

[3]The figure rises to over 50 per cent if a foreign language is excluded.

This argument takes us right back to the case we want to make for the curriculum as an 'entitlement to knowledge'. Of course the children of richer parents have enormous advantages in our society and it is undeniable that schools able to charge £30,000 or more a year in fees are selective in the pupils they take. However, this is an issue about distribution of wealth and the social selection that this makes possible; it is about elitist schools, not necessarily an elitist curriculum. The knowledge on which maths or history as GCSE subjects is based is not a 'cultural arbitrary' as the sociologist Pierre Bourdieu once claimed. It has a form of universality derived from two sources: (a) how mathematics has been developed by specialists in the universities, and (b) how school maths teachers select and sequence mathematics content in ways that their theory and experience tells them is appropriate for the majority of pupils at different ages. We would not be doing a service to those students who struggle with maths, history or any other subject by reducing the more difficult content of some subjects or by treating physics as equivalent to leisure and tourism.

Our argument in this book is that teachers who want to improve the achievement of their pupils have two strategies in relation to reducing inequalities. One is internal and pedagogic and the other is external and political. For a school their internal pedagogic strategy will have two aspects – at a school level the head will endeavour to improve the qualifications of her or his subject departments when recruiting new staff and by supporting existing staff to undertake further studies as the basis for improving the curriculum. At the departmental level, the focus will be pedagogic; teachers will be encouraged to attend courses to upgrade their specialist pedagogic knowledge. The role of subjects and the subject departments in a school's curriculum is an issue we return to in Chapters 4 and 7. The unequal distribution of educational resources raises political questions relevant to teachers as members of political parties but not in their role as members of staff of individual schools. As citizens in a democracy, teachers may choose to get involved politically at the local or national level to try and influence government educational policy. That is distinct though not unrelated to their role in the school as members of the teaching profession.

We cannot exclude the possibility that a school adopting a stronger knowledge-led curriculum could find this led to a drop in examination results although not necessarily a fall in standards. This is where the curriculum leadership role of the head becomes crucial. She or he would have to convince the governors, first, that there were other measures of standards than examination grades and, secondly, that in the longer term, a stronger emphasis on the 'entitlement to knowledge' will lead to higher standards and more examination successes.

One response to the standards issue is to take a historical perspective. There is space here for only a very brief sketch but it is important because it reminds us of the incremental nature of educational change. Despite the many difficulties that schools face today in reducing inequalities, when we look back to the 1944 Education Act and to the nearly 70 years of 'secondary education for all' that have followed, we see a 'success story', rather than a story of failure. The most dramatic evidence of success is the proportion of young people who now go to university; it has increased at least ten times in those 70 years; that cannot be anything but evidence of 'success'. It is a major achievement of generations of teachers which has not always received the recognition it deserves and is a good starting point for thinking about the goals of the school curriculum for what we refer to in the title of this book as *future schools*. If we extrapolate from 1944, our starting point for thinking about future schools might be that by 2084, 80 per cent of each cohort would go to university or have the qualifications for entry that they might use later in their lives. This is not so unrealistic when we remember that the proportion of current cohorts entering higher education in Finland is already over 60 per cent. Any just curriculum for a future school must surely envisage making such a future possible.

The curriculum and 'future schools'

A focus on education as the *entitlement to knowledge* allows us to identify some of the conditions that are most likely to ensure the continued expansion and better distribution of educational opportunities. It also enables us to identify how well-intentioned recent policies have led us astray. A key example of such a policy is the assumption of the previous government that widening participation and more students obtaining more certificates that were treated as equivalent to GCSEs necessarily meant that educational opportunities were being extended.

Entitlement should result in access; however, the idea of 'access' becomes empty of meaning unless we ask the question 'access to what'. Our understanding of the purpose of schools suggests that while widening access is an important starting principle, it is inadequate on its own without a curriculum criterion. A curriculum must provide access to 'knowledge' – not to 'facts', and not to 'learning' unless what is to be learned is specified. We have found it useful to use the narrower term 'epistemic access' when referring to the curriculum. The question that the idea of 'epistemic access' poses for all schools and all subject teachers is 'does your curriculum help *all students* to shape and guide their learning in the search for truth' whatever course they are on and whatever the subject they are studying, vocational or academic. Like knowledge, truth is another difficult and misunderstood word and certainly we do not mean truth in an absolute sense. We mean the best truth a student can grasp depending on their age and development. Furthermore, truth is like knowledge; it is differentiated and may be scientific, aesthetic, moral or practical. Somehow, as teachers, in whatever we ask our students to do – there should be some idea in our mind that it has a 'truthful' outcome or challenge to existing ideas – it might be about a poem, a historical source or the property of a chemical element. That challenge to a student's existing ideas is what 'epistemic access' refers to.

Subjects and the curriculum

The current government's curriculum and examination reforms place far more emphasis on school subjects as the basis of the curriculum than the policies of its predecessors. The arguments for and against a subject-based curriculum are hotly debated and we will return to them in some detail in Chapters 4 and 7. However there are issues involved in establishing a National Curriculum that are important, whether or not the current reforms are supported.

The first is the assumption that a National Curriculum makes that there is 'universal' or 'better' knowledge (although in subjects such as history and literature this 'universality' will be expressed differently in different countries). The second is that a National Curriculum expresses the entitlement to that knowledge for *all children* in a country, regardless of their different social and cultural experiences outside school. The present Secretary of State for England expresses this entitlement in terms of *having high expectations for all children*. This is an important principle; however it is difficult to take seriously when at the same time, the new National Curriculum does not apply to academies (the majority of secondary schools) and government funded 'free' schools. Is there an assumption on the part of government that making a school an academy (and independent of a local authority) in some way guarantees the entitlement that is only guaranteed by the National Curriculum for other schools?

As educational specialists, our role with all those working in the schools is to specify the conditions for realizing high expectations for as large a proportion of each cohort as possible. It is this role that makes us 'knowledge specialists', or in more familiar terms, curriculum specialists. This does not make us specialists in all the different subjects that make up a school curriculum. However, the idea of entitlement or 'high expectations *for all children*' assumes that these expectations are the same for all children regardless of their social, ethnic background or gender. Why is this important and why does it present such a challenge both to teachers and to government?

This question can be answered in several ways. Teachers have to face the reality that despite starting with 'high expectations for all pupils', not all pupils fulfil these expectations – some get poor grades and some fail. Individual teachers, schools and the government inevitably look for explanations. Some blame each other or the pupils and their families and researchers devote much time to trying to work out which factor appears to be more important. We do not deny any of the obvious factors: inadequate distribution of resources, poor pedagogy and underqualified teachers, difficult family circumstances and individual pupil learning difficulties or lack of motivation. Research has swung unhelpfully between the poles of 'schools do matter' and 'the causes of differences are largely external to the schools'. In this book we take a different – and we hope more constructive, although not easier – approach that starts from the knowledge that all pupils are entitled to. It can be summarized briefly as follows:

- There is agreed 'powerful knowledge'.

- A school has responsibility for ensuring that that all students have access to the foundations of powerful knowledge[4] and that there are opportunities for those who have not achieved to a level equivalent to the EBacc by the age of 16 to continue their foundation studies as part of any post-16 programme they take.

- Each school and the country as a whole (and its government) should constantly review the gap between the 'entitlement to knowledge' and the reality of differential achievement. They should collectively take responsibility for their role in realizing the aims of 'entitlement for all'.

---

[4]The EBacc is an initial attempt to express what such foundations might involve.

- No school should be held responsible for failures that are beyond its control. For example, there will be factors in the local community or region and related to the background experiences of their pupils that schools have little control over. Likewise the responsibilities and control of governments are limited. They can influence the availability of teachers with good specialist qualifications; however, the relative autonomy of individual schools will be used in different ways.

- The factors over which individual schools have increasing control are a school's curriculum and its teachers' approach to pedagogy. We will return to these issues later in this book.

The key distinguishing feature of a knowledge-led curriculum based on an 'entitlement to knowledge' is that the issue of the knowledge a school wants its pupils to have access to is its starting point. As we argue in Chapter 2, a knowledge-led curriculum must be defined by subjects and the proportion of the school week that they are assigned. This stands in sharp contrast to the idea that the school curriculum should start with the interests and experiences of the children, their parents and the locality, or with broad ideas such as well-being. Examples of this approach which for us are well intentioned but seriously mistaken are the RSA's popular Opening Minds and local curriculum programmes. It is not that such programmes do not recognize that knowledge is important, or that interdisciplinary studies do not have a role to play. There are at least two problems involved in placing an emphasis in the curriculum on locality and pupil experiences. First, it weakens the role of subjects as the basis for ensuring that students progress and do not miss out on key concepts; and secondly, as a recent Bristol study showed, schools in lower income areas are far more likely to opt for programmes based on local experience than schools in higher income areas.

We do not under-value pupil experience of the locality of a school. As we argue in Chapters 5 and 7, for example, pupil experiences of where they live are a crucial resource for teachers. Nor does a knowledge-led curriculum imply that every child in a school will acquire the same knowledge at the same pace. What a knowledge-led curriculum does do, which sets it apart from the RSA programmes, is to place the 'entitlement to knowledge' as the starting point of the curriculum for all children.

The entitlement to knowledge

The idea that every pupil has an 'entitlement to knowledge', and indeed that this is the only basis for continuing to expand educational opportunities, rests on two assumptions. The first assumption, touched on earlier in this chapter, is that, albeit in different ways in different fields, there is *better knowledge* – the Russian psychologist Lev Vygotsky called it *higher order thinking*. A similar view was expressed by the English sociologist, Basil Bernstein. In critiquing forms of compensatory education which excluded pupils from discipline-based knowledge, he argued that academic disciplines were the 'public forms of understanding through which a society has conversations about itself and its future'. We do not mean *better* in the sense that it is knowledge beyond debate, nor that better knowledge in any field is 'fixed' as in the nineteenth-century 'liberal curriculum' and its reliance on the Classics of Ancient Greece and Rome. *Better knowledge* means the best knowledge we have and the best means we have for creating new knowledge for the kind of world we envisage for the next generation. In fields such as the humanities and most of the social sciences it will mean access to the different ways of thinking about social, historical or geographical phenomena – Chapter 7 illustrates this in the case of geography. Despite the lack of consensus among social scientists and humanities teachers, some concept of a 'canon' for these subjects seems an inescapable feature of any national curriculum. In contrast, mathematics and the natural sciences, at school level, will be less about debates and different interpretations and more about what existing knowledge tells us about the natural and physical worlds. The important point about a knowledge-led school curriculum is that it relies on the 'best' ideas and enquiries of the specialist communities which give priority to discovering, debating, testing and evaluating new knowledge – whether scientific laws, novels or engineering designs. Chapter 3 explains why we find it helpful to refer to this 'best knowledge' as *powerful knowledge* and what this means as a principle for the curriculum. Chapter 4 develops this argument about knowledge – why it points to a subject-based curriculum and what its practical implications may be for headteachers and subject specialists in schools. Given that our experience is largely about secondary education, this book focuses on secondary rather than on primary schools. However, our argument is that making knowledge the starting point for the curriculum is no less relevant to those working in primary schools. We do not make schooling compulsory for all 5 year olds just to extend their experience – we want their schooling to give them access to knowledge that takes them beyond that experience in ways they and their parents can trust and value, that they will find exciting and challenging and which prepares them for the next stage of their education – secondary school. It is, to put it mildly, ironic that the only schools in England that are explicitly referred to as 'preparatory' are the private fee-charging schools which 'prepare' students for private, fee-paying secondary schools which even more ironically, we call 'Public'. For us it makes sense that all schools are 'preparatory' – in other words in focusing on the 'development' of children they have a view of a child's possible future in mind in ways that reflect the age of their pupils. This in no way denies a place for play in schools for younger pupils and for its expression as sport and other 'extra curricular' activities when they get older.

This chapter began by asserting that this is not a 'how to' book, nor is it a book of educational theory and full of references to journal articles that few have time to read.[5] Starting from the assumption that the purpose of schools is to support the 'entitlement to knowledge', it presents ways of thinking about the question 'what do we teach?' at every level from national curriculum policy to school leadership teams to classroom practice.

Responding to the current reforms

We nail our colours firmly to the 'mast' that *all pupils* are entitled to what we refer to as 'powerful knowledge', as an educational goal and

[5]We have added some suggestions for additional reading for those who want to take these ideas further.

as a principle of educational justice. This is easy to say or write but far from easy to accomplish. The strong emphasis on knowledge that is expressed in the government's current reforms is often seen as being more likely to lead to pupil disaffection and failure than to enhancing their achievements or commitment to learning. This is a challenge that schools have to face directly and there are no easy solutions. It is not surprising that one response to the government's reforms is that they must be resisted in any way possible. The reforms are seen as elitist, backward looking, neglect all the 'progress' that teachers have made in the past decades and pay scant regard to any research. Some critics go so far as claiming that in their total disregard for the experience and views of most of the specialist educational community, the reforms rely on little more than the personal prejudices of the Secretary of State. This book sympathizes with these reactions to the top-down way in which the present government's reforms have been introduced; it is almost as if they were presented as Michael Gove's personal preferences. However, we see no good educational purpose in focusing on the personal political style of the Secretary of State. We see the type of critical response to his reforms and the degree of support such criticisms have gained as a symptom of how far the broader educational culture has turned against knowledge. It is as if being 'for knowledge' is the same as being 'for Michael Gove' and vice versa. There is a real danger in being trapped in this 'for' or 'against' debate about the government's reforms when far more important and fundamental issues of educational justice are at stake. Social class differences in achievement, in access to top universities and in entry into the professions have increased not decreased in the past decade. This is confirmed time and again by the data on social mobility. This may not be the direct result of past curriculum reforms; however, it is inconceivable that such trends to greater inequality will be reversed if a knowledge-led curriculum is not extended to the majority.

How is it that anti-knowledge views of the curriculum and schooling have become dominant in university educational faculties even more than in schools and that the idea of a knowledge-led curriculum is seen as an elitist and exclusive and not as a right of all pupils? It is an attitude that would be unthinkable in France, Germany or in most if not all other European countries. This introductory chapter concludes with a very brief history of why in this country there are such negative responses within the education community to the idea of 'a common entitlement to knowledge for all' and how we might have reached such an impasse.

For and against knowledge-led schools: A brief history

The expansion of our public education system in England has been torn between two well-intentioned but ultimately divisive approaches to the curriculum. One has been based on a concept of excellence associated with the idea of liberal education which was gradually extended from the 'Public' schools to the grammar schools and with the reorganization of secondary education from 1965, was incorporated into the upper streams of comprehensive schools. This is often symbolized by Matthew Arnold's famous phrase 'The best which has been thought and said.' Although Arnold was deeply committed to education for all, and spent his whole life inspecting schools for the children of the poorest sections of society, his emphasis on 'the best' is often taken as a sign of his elitism. Commenting on the charge that Arnold was an elitist is beyond the scope of this book. What is undoubtedly true is that for all his concern to improve the education of the poor, his concept of 'culture for all' was rooted in the classics and gave scant reference to the way the society of his time was being transformed by innovations in science and technology. His conservative and backward-looking view of the curriculum was a benign and 'in spirit' at least, egalitarian example of what, in the next chapter we shall call Future 1.

Since 1944, when secondary education for all became enshrined in statute, and in particular since 1988 when the first National Curriculum was established, England has made successive but only partially successful attempts to update Matthew Arnold's ideas as a principle for 'education for all'. The expansion of access to higher education can be seen as an indication of the relative success of these attempts. What has hardly been addressed is whether the public/grammar 'liberal education' school curriculum is in some way intrinsically elitist or whether it might be the basis of a curriculum entitlement for all. The Coalition government's reforms since 2010 propose a return to a version of an Arnoldian Future 1 view of culture and a 'curriculum for all'. At the same time they show far less concern than Arnold did with the consequences for the less than half of each cohort who are in no way prepared for their future in an increasingly complex, global knowledge-led economy and a world which faces severe ecological and environmental challenges. Insofar as the government addresses this question, success or failure appears to be seen almost entirely in individual terms – those who are motivated will succeed and the rest either do not deserve to succeed or lack the ability. Of course, individual motivation is important; however, such a focus on the individual student does not take us very far from Margaret Thatcher's 'there is no such thing as society' – hardly an adequate recipe for innovation and a growing economy, let alone a more just society.

The second approach had its origins in a rejection both of the narrowness of the elementary school tradition of '3 R's' (Reading, (W)riting and (A)rithmetic) and of Arnold's 'best' as being in effect no more than best as seen 'by the few and for the few'. It can be can be traced back to the reforms of the 1920s and 1930s but took its modern expression in the 1960s with the Newsom Report – aptly titled *Half Our Future*. Newsom argued that we should not start from a view of a common curriculum for all, but from the pupils themselves, their interests and their likely future in other words, their culture. This led to well-intentioned attempts to build curricula around the diverse interests of those identified as 'non-academic children' and the communities they came from; a kind of 'localism'. The first examples were the programmes proposed by the then Schools Council with titles such as *Science for the Young School Leaver, Geography for the Young School Leaver* and *Mathematics for the Majority*. These new curricula, followed by TVEI (the Technical and Vocational Initiative) in the 1980s were taken up by teachers in often highly innovative ways that were not always tied to the Newsom Report's divisive cultural assumptions – school-based curricula and assessment were only some of the many innovations that the Newsom Report and the schools council funding that followed, led to. However the titles of these early programmes – for the young school leaver – masked a reality that was systematically avoided. They assumed that there were two kinds of geography and two kinds of history, mathematics and science – each as valuable as the other but for different groups in society; one kind for those who were expected to stay on at school after the age of 16 and progress to university and the other kind for 'the rest'. This divided approach to the curriculum has continued both in the differentiated forms of assessment for GCSE, less overtly in the RSA's Opening Minds and Area-based Curriculum Projects mentioned earlier and in the recent Demos Report, *The Forgotten Half* (2011) which echoes the title of Newsom's Report 50 years earlier. There is a danger that such assumptions could be repeated in the Labour Party's proposals for a Tech Bac. All continue with the philosophy of giving priority to the motivations of students and links with their somewhat hypothetical future employment possibilities. By implication, at least, they assume that access to 'real knowledge' is beyond them.

The Coalition government when elected in 2010 dismissed all previous attempts to mask curricula differences by laying down a curriculum based on subject knowledge that is designed to be a benchmark for *all* students up to the age of 16; their proposals impose strict criteria for treating subjects and forms of assessment as equivalent. At the same time, they have given little attention to what might be involved for the less motivated students, if a subject-based curriculum, at least up to 16, was to include all of each cohort.

In the context of the challenges posed by such reforms, the 'fear of' or even 'rejection of knowledge' by teachers referred to earlier is understandable. Nor is it surprising that these fears are given some legitimacy by being associated with certain fashionable trends in educational theory that call into question the very idea that there can, objectively, be 'better' knowledge. At least the more comfortable alternative of a learner and experience-led curriculum that New Labour and the Qualifications and Curriculum Development Authority (QCDA) offered following the 2008 National Curriculum was less likely to be experienced as an 'imposition' on pupils. The current battle between many sections of the educational community and the government is not a productive one – both lead in different ways to an educational underclass with few resources but their wits and the possibility of a few sporting or pop music successes.

The alternative approach to the curriculum suggested in this book owes a debt to the Italian activist and political and educational theorist, Antonio Gramsci, who died in one of Mussolini's prisons nearly 80 years ago. It is interesting that while Gramsci's political ideas have been long endorsed by the Left, they have, with a few exceptions, largely neglected his educational philosophy. On the other hand the importance of his educational ideas is acknowledged by Michael Gove, the current Secretary of State and his educational mentor, the American E. D. Hirsch, both of whom managed to void their political implications. It maybe that the potential contradiction in the title of Harold Entwistle's seminal intellectual biography – Antonio Gramsci: *Conservative Schooling for Radical Politics* – was more prescient than even Entwistle knew.

In emphasizing the concept of 'entitlement to knowledge for all', this book offers an alternative way of thinking about the curriculum rather than a way out of the dilemma facing schools and teachers in a society that is characterized by inequalities. It suggests how present government reforms might be used for sound educational ends rather than just rejected. It also addresses government but in a different way. To them it says 'if you are serious about building a system based on high expectations for all, this requires a redistribution of resources that as yet we see no sign of'. The gap between universalizing the criteria for knowledge which is endorsed by the government and the far from universal distribution of opportunities for accessing such knowledge raises difficult political questions in a time of public spending austerity. It raises equally difficult pedagogic and curriculum issues for heads and classroom teachers, educational researchers and teacher educators which are no less avoidable. Under New Labour the QCDA introduced a framework of levels which classified academic and non-academic subjects as equivalent. Lower achieving students were advised to take the non-academic courses; however, while in some cases this led them to higher level courses and even to employment, most did not. By and large teachers went along with this; the question we raise is 'was this social justice?'

In this book we argue that social and more explicitly curricula justice is inescapably linked to the widest possible access to what we refer to as 'powerful knowledge' and that schools and their curricula are the main instrument through which this can be achieved. The aim of the book is to make explicit what we mean by 'powerful knowledge' and why it should be the basis for a universal entitlement for all. As this introductory chapter has indicated, this issue has been implicit though rarely explicitly debated in every reform of the past century. Since the election of the present government, this issue has surfaced more explicitly than ever before in sharp disagreements between the educational community and the current Secretary of State. This book is an attempt to offer a way beyond these disagreements for how headteachers and schools might think about their curriculum and realize the old Enlightenment goal that schooling should be an 'entitlement to knowledge for all'.

2

Why start with the curriculum?

Michael Young

Introduction

In revising an earlier draft of this chapter, I immediately faced a problem[1] which in a way is a problem for this book as a whole. As Carolyn and Martin Roberts say in the Preface 'what matters most (and what this book is about) is the curriculum'. On the other hand, it is doubtful whether for many heads such questions as 'what is the knowledge that we want all students to have access to?' would come top of their agenda for discussions with their staff. More likely they would give their primary attention to external examinations and how to get more of their students achieving a C rather than a D grade in maths or English. Furthermore, they could reasonably argue that this was the best contribution they could make both to raising standards and to more equal system. It is hard to disagree, at least in the short term, that schools can

---

[1]Pointed out to me most perceptively by John Morgan, Professor of Curriculum at the University of Auckland, New Zealand.

or should suddenly drop all interest in improving grades, far from it. We want to argue that in 'theory' (in this chapter) and in 'practice' (see Chapters 5 and 6) there are sound educational reasons for heads and their staff to take the curriculum as their starting point and look beyond immediate assessment issues. Governments are always going to overemphasize assessment and league tables. However, the only way any government is going to learn that this is a mistaken approach to improving standards is if heads and teachers as 'educational specialists' in schools and as well as those in education faculties are clear why this is so and what an alternative less assessment oriented approach would look like.

Why then do we argue that it is the *curriculum* and not assessment and examinations that matters most in making a successful school? And why, as I will take further in the next chapter, is it important to separate curriculum and pedagogy when for teachers in classrooms, studios, labs and workshops, they inescapably come together?

In Chapter 7, David Lambert suggests that 'curriculum' is probably the most distinctive *educational* idea that we have. Hospitals, factories, law courts and families, to name a few institutions, do not have curricula; it is only schools (and of course, colleges and universities[2]). It is the curriculum that pupils immediately recognize as making schools different from the rest of their experience even if they have never heard of the word. What they do find in schools is teachers who in systematic ways, from term to term and year following year, plan how they are going to encourage and enable

---

[2]It is only recently that college and university curricula have begun to be the subject of debate and research.

their students to develop their knowledge. It is the knowledge that teachers want students to acquire that defines the curriculum, how they do this is what we refer to as pedagogy[3] and how they reflect on whether they are successful is why assessment is always part of any teacher's pedagogy. As public institutions, schools rely on the trust of their public – parents, tax payers, voters and government. It is that trust that is or should be *supported by* and not *driven by* external instruments like examinations. Examinations provide necessary information to governments, parents, employers and to teachers and pupils themselves. However, examinations defeat their purposes for everyone if, instead of supporting the professional judgements of teachers, they come to displace them. The more the purposes of schools and the professionalism of teachers have public support, the more external examinations will support teachers rather than determine what they do. It is worth citing two models that might serve as examples of where this public trust in professionalism and shared purposes is most apparent and where the curriculum purposes rather than external evaluation is given priority. One is the doctorate (or Ph.D.) awarded by universities for a 'contribution to new knowledge' in a specialist field. In the case of doctorates, public trust is placed in the specialist academic communities in the universities involved in producing new knowledge in different fields. This case is illustrative; it is not claiming that this autonomy of the universities is directly or immediately applicable to schools. My second example is the widely respected German Abitur, the

---

[3]It is interesting that pedagogy is in a way an idea that is less specific to schools (and of course colleges and universities) than curriculum. Both management and therapy embody an element of pedagogy but it would be hard to say they involve a curriculum.

certificate, similar to A levels but broader in curriculum that was referred to in the Introduction. Students achieve an Abitur at the age of 18 or 19 on completion of their secondary schooling and it is assessed by teachers of individual schools, not by external examinations. The professional communities in each of the cases, university teachers and school teachers, are trusted by the public to guarantee standards and quality. That level of public trust which is similar to that found for accountants, lawyers and other professions is a situation that we should work towards for our schools. It requires agreement on the purpose of teaching as a profession – and in the case of teaching it is expressed by the curriculum and its links with teacher expertise. However achieving such trust will be a long road. At present the trust between government and teachers is low; hence the emphasis on external control through examinations and inspection.

The curriculum is not, therefore just one of the many things a head has responsibility for – it defines the purposes of a school and the journey a school wants its pupils to take.

The context of current curriculum reforms

As I said in the previous chapter, I do not intend to enter into the broader political debates about government policies: like any citizen, I have my personal views. I aim to approach the question of the curriculum and 'what is taught in schools' as an educational specialist, or more specifically as a curriculum theorist. At the same time, I recognize that my approach cannot be completely separate from my personal values.

Much of the current debate is overpoliticized. As a result it easily neglects that there are real educational issues about what schools are for, and why so many pupils do not, in any terms, get a 'good education'. Furthermore, despite the pressures on schools of recent reforms there are also developments that leave schools more on their own than ever before. If these developments are looked at positively, schools have more opportunities for deciding what they offer their pupils than they have had since the launching of the National Curriculum, whether they are responsible to a local education authority, a group managing academies or the governors of a free school. The abolition of the QCDA (and though of less significance, BECTA and the GTC[4]), together with the more limited subject specifications of the new National Curriculum, will give more autonomy to individual schools and their heads and therefore require them to be much more explicit about their own curriculum priorities. There are parallels with the potentially greater influence of GP's as a consequence of the new approach to commissioning hospital care. However, if this shift in responsibility for 'what is taught in schools' is to become a reality and not just remain little more than rhetoric, it will make considerable new demands on individual headteachers and their staff. The government appears to be saying to schools, although not explicitly, 'you are the curriculum specialists, it is up to you'. This change will involve much more than management and much more than budgetary control, although both are of course important. If schools are to define and own their own purposes it is to the curriculum that they must turn, whether or not that involves

---

[4]The Qualifications and Curriculum Authority, the British Educational Computing and Technology Agency and the General Teaching Council.

interpreting the specifications of the National Curriculum in the case of schools that are part of local education authorities, or developing their own curriculum in the case of academies. That is why we stress leadership in this book, and specifically curriculum leadership. To put it more concretely, each school will need to develop a shared vision about what it teaches, when and how, about what exams to enter their students for and when it is educationally sound to allow pupils of different ages to make choices about what they study.

Curriculum leadership and the issue of choice

Choice has become a fashionable but easily misunderstood slogan in education in recent years. In a general sense, no one can be against increased 'choice'; it is part of what being in a democracy is about. However, the choices we have a right to, and can or should make are not all the same. There is no complex issue involved in choosing what to buy in a supermarket; however some choices are only real if the chooser has the knowledge about the implications of different choices. We do not, on the whole, expect to 'choose' which drug to take when we are ill. In education, it is right that parents have more choice than in the past over which school to send their children to.[5] On the other hand, when it comes to the curriculum, pupils (as well as their parents) often lack the knowledge to make the best choices in terms of pupils' future. It is as if the market and the idea that

---

[5]In a country like Finland where the standards and reputations of schools vary little, there is little school choice because it is taken for granted that all schools are good.

the individual always makes the best choices for herself or himself has been extended far beyond where it is appropriate. We expect our doctors, our lawyers and our accountants to listen to us but not necessarily to say 'it is up to you'. Like members of these and other professions, teachers are experts in their field, although this does not of course mean they are always right. Furthermore, a teacher's field of expertise is much broader than classroom teaching. It extends to interpreting what a school's curriculum can offer to pupils, parents and to employers and in making professional judgements in advising pupils and their parents about the best decisions that they can make about their education. Pupils, parents and (where relevant) employers are, in a sense, 'clients' of schools, and like all relationships between clients and members of professions, their relationships are based on trust. As in the case of all professions, it is trust in the specialist knowledge of the particular profession that we as 'clients' rely on. This means not only that teachers have responsibility for educating their pupils but also for educating (in the broader sense) their pupils' parents and the wider community about what their school can offer their pupils. It is because we recognize the professional knowledge of teachers that our society gives schools responsibility for their curricula as well as the day-to-day activities of classrooms over which they have direct control.

Since 1988 and the launch of the first National Curriculum in England, it has been reviewed and revised by governments of both major political parties, sometimes in response to pressures from teachers as in the 1990s and sometimes in direct opposition to many teachers in the case of the recent reforms. Successive labour governments after 1997 attempted to modernize the National

Curriculum and this involved the QCDA making more and more suggestions to teachers about what they should do and Ofsted tended to evaluate the schools and the teachers rather than the curriculum. Both developments effectively minimized the professional role of teachers and their curriculum expertise.

In the current reforms, despite being widely opposed both by teachers and the wider education community, the National Curriculum takes on more of the role of national guidelines, and it is a real opportunity for teachers and schools to recognize their role as curriculum specialists, by interpreting these guidelines for their school. A National Curriculum expressed as guidelines relies on each school to develop its own curriculum. What becomes increasingly important is the distinction between *the* National Curriculum as a set of guidelines and how schools interpret these guidelines in developing *their* curriculum.

Carolyn Roberts in Chapter 6 gives an example of how her school, drawing on some of the ideas in this book, developed what she describes as its knowledge-led curriculum.

The question, therefore, that this chapter asks, is what is this specialist curriculum knowledge that teachers, at least in principle should be able to draw on in developing their school curriculum, whether or not their school is bound by the National Curriculum? It is this specialist knowledge that I refer to as *curriculum theory*.

Why is a curriculum theory necessary?

It was long ago now that the curriculum theorist Lawrence Stenhouse reminded us that there is no curriculum development without teacher development. Although this remains an important insight, it was open to misinterpretation and to the neglect, or at least the playing down of an important issue. If teachers are to be as integral to the curriculum as any profession should be about its major priorities, they need *professional knowledge* – in other words a theory of the curriculum, or more concretely, a theory of the knowledge their students are entitled to during their time at school. Without such a theory, they will be left with either their personal opinions or 'transmitting' what is laid down for them by others. Teaching is a specialist activity and specialization involves practice, experience and knowledge – the kind of specialist knowledge associated with all professions which most people, especially in the case of teaching, pupils and parents, do not have. Teaching is not a mere formalized version of a parent telling a child or what he or she should do in particular circumstances (like a supermarket manager telling someone taking over a check out what she or he should do, for example). It took me a long time to realize the implications of this difference and its implications for my role as a 'curriculum theorist'. It is not, as I once thought, just to analyse and criticize existing curricula – although it involves both. Nor is it to tell teachers what to do in a particular class. Not only would a university-based curriculum theorist never have the necessary knowledge of the particular class and pupils, but it would undermine the professionalism of teachers. The role of curriculum theory must be to develop ideas about what is important for young people to learn and how – and so to be a potential resource for teachers and headteachers in their roles as curriculum specialists.

Practice without theory: Some examples

Some readers will remember or have read about the William Tyndale School affair. William Tyndale is a primary school in North London; in the 1970s the teachers followed a 'learner-centred' approach to the curriculum, which, to be fair to them was only a logical extension of the child-centred ideas they would have been likely to have picked up on teacher training courses. However, as soon as one thinks of a headteacher being not just a manager but a curriculum leader faced with responsibility for her or his school's curriculum, the inadequacy of the idea of such a learner-centred curriculum becomes apparent.

How could the children know what they should learn when they come to school? The irony and one of the reasons why the William Tyndale affair became such a 'cause celebre' was that the teachers linked their child-centred model of schooling to their socialist politics. It was as if, somehow, by freeing their pupils from a curriculum they were agents of radical social change, rather than denying them access to knowledge. Some years earlier, I applied for a post as head of science in a comprehensive school with a head who shared many of the educational ideas of the William Tyndale teachers. The first thing he said to me after offering me the job was 'Remember, when pupils complain about a teacher, I always put the students views first.' I turned the job down; how could I be a head of a science department, if the head gave more authority to the pupils who came to school almost certainly knowing no science than to his specialist science teachers. It was then that I began to grasp that there was something fundamentally wrong with the idea of teachers putting learners at the centre of the curriculum. Schools and their teachers need to know where their students are coming from, what their interests are and what their experiences have been. However, a teacher's primary focus must be not on what they already know but on the journey they hope their pupils will make while they are at the school.

The next section of this chapter addresses how we might think about this journey and I explain why I came to see that a pupil's journey 'through the curriculum' must be shaped by the knowledge we want them to have access to and, using a term I have already referred to, why this knowledge must as far as possible be 'powerful knowledge'. It is identifying what knowledge is powerful for pupils at different ages that, I argue, is one of the major professional tasks of teachers. However, they are not alone; there is (or should be) the guidelines of a National Curriculum and the subjects that they have specialized in when studying at university to draw on. They also need to develop their specialist knowledge in how students can be helped to acquire subject knowledge that they may initially experience as alien to them. This specialist pedagogic knowledge is no less complex or difficult than subject knowledge itself – whether, to take three examples, this is history, physics or accountancy.

From theory to curriculum: Lessons from the 1970's sociology of education

In this section, I start by recalling how I was led to the idea of 'powerful knowledge' as the basis of any school curriculum. It was, to put it mildly, a troubled journey. My first job after leaving school teaching was to lecture in sociology of education – to teachers and student teachers. My task, as I saw it at the time, was to show students how any educational process, whether it was the selection of students by IQ tests, teaching, assessing students or making curriculum decisions, masked a set of power relations. Initially I, like many of my students at the time, found this an exciting and radical approach. If we could only see society and its institutions as power relations, and convince those without power of the truth of this argument we would have the basis of making a much fairer, more equal and more just society. My task was to introduce my students who were to be teachers, to these ideas. But who was going to seize this opportunity to redistribute power. Surely not, as some thought, teachers with their students in classrooms? Karl Marx thought it was the working class, although there was little sign of it at the time; radicalized teachers in the 1970s extended Marx's concept of the working class to students, women, ethnic minorities, teachers and ultimately to children. However, it soon became clear that, attractive though such ideas seemed to be, they had little (or at best, a short-lived) link to the reality of the time, in political or educational terms. My personal response was to become sceptical of the theory[6] as little more than an academic debate with no connection to real life. It led me to give up the sociology of education and become involved in what I hoped were more practical policies designed to help those who left school without any examination passes and any prospect

---

[6]These developments played some part in justifying the removal of sociology of education, and later, any broader study of education, from the initial training of teachers.

of a job. Not exactly a realistic task as the persistent unemployment of 16–19 year olds has since proved but at least it seemed more 'grounded' in reality.

The limits of critique: Lessons from post-apartheid South Africa

Working on policies for young people with no qualifications led me to think more about a qualification system that denied recognition to so many young people. This led to several invitations to visit South Africa during the period between the release of Nelson Mandela from prison in 1990 and his election as president in 1995.

One of the major tasks of the recently legalized democratic movement in South Africa was to develop a blue print for the kind of education system they wanted to replace the racially segregated system that they had inherited from apartheid. Many good things were achieved at the time: non-racist national and provincial forms of government (they replaced 18 racially divided Departments of Education!!) and a broad vision of education for *all* children regardless of ethnic background or gender. However when it came to what such a vision might mean for the curriculum, things were not so straightforward. The only clear policies being proposed by progressive educational researchers like myself were to free teachers from the hierarchical and racially divided curriculum associated with apartheid and link this 'freedom' to a set of outcomes based on the visionary goals of the ANC for a democratic and socially just South Africa. What emerged was a set of broad statements of educational outcomes not unlike those adopted in countries such as Scotland and New Zealand and in England at the beginning of the year 2000 and described by Carolyn Roberts in the early part of Chapter 6. However, South Africa was very different from such countries. It inherited largely weak institutions except for the children of the white elite and minimally trained teachers whose only professional experience had been of the rigidly controlled apartheid system. Not surprisingly they found the new 'freedom' completely beyond them. They literally did not know what to do. Following a series of reviews, South African education has been suffering from (and slowly recovering from) this disastrous situation ever since.

There are two reasons why I mention the South African case in this chapter. One is that it highlights in highly dramatic way, the consequences of implementing an approach to the curriculum that is based only on critique and relies on a set of very broad outcomes to express the needs and interests of all learners. In South Africa, the project of freeing pupils and teachers from a curriculum was an understandable reaction to the experience of being dictated to by an elite dedicated to suppressing their rights. What is disturbing is that the freedom was extended to opposing any curriculum that sets out 'essential knowledge' so that the idea of knowledge itself comes to be seen as something imposed and either to be feared or resisted. The assumption that such ideas are based on is that no knowledge is 'better' or more worth knowing. Unless it was the free product of the interaction between teachers and pupils it was inevitably seen as a form of domination. Lists of outcomes, it was hoped, could guide teachers and replace the previous subject syllabuses which were seen as arbitrary and unrelated to anything in the experience of all but a minority of pupils. In South Africa, the sense of political freedom associated with the abolition of apartheid was extended to education, at least in schools in the most disadvantaged areas; it was as if the right to an education was as simple as the right to vote. The South African situation, for me and increasing numbers of South Africans, dramatized the inadequacy of any curriculum that did not start with the knowledge that pupils in a democratic country are entitled to.

The second reason for mentioning the South African case is that very similar ideas, expressed in a more theoretical form, of teachers and pupils co-constructing knowledge were also the ideas that made my first book, *Knowledge and Control*, such a success, especially as an Open University set text for teachers studying for a degree. I have frequently met teachers in this and other countries who tell me how such ideas had changed their lives. They had clearly 'touched a cord' in teachers' sense of identity as members of a profession who wanted but were unable, in the schools that they found themselves in, to express their care and commitment to children and their learning. However, the situation in this country, with teachers far better educated and schools with far more resources, was very different from South Africa. It took the extreme circumstances of a country trying to find its way out of the rigid and racist system of apartheid for me to realize that something was wrong with the ideas if they persuaded teachers to dismiss the importance of knowledge as a basis for taking pupils beyond their experience. However, at the time I could not work out what the underlying problem was.

Lessons from theory

Back in England in the late 1990s, and not long after the curriculum reforms in South Africa that I referred to, an article[7] was published which sharply criticized my earlier work and its assumption that the curriculum was little more than the ideas of those groups with power in a society. The two researchers were colleagues of mine who I respected, and although I did not like their criticisms at the time, I was unable to dismiss them. They understood the ideas all too well and it was not insignificant that one of the authors, Johan Muller, was South African, and he had witnessed the devastating impact of the rejection of knowledge on the schools in post-apartheid South Africa. What I learned from his paper with Rob Moore was that a theory that equates the curriculum with the imposition of 'knowledge' defined by those with power – 'knowledge of the powerful' as I came to refer to it – leaves teachers and curriculum designers with no curriculum at all.

Rescuing the curriculum from its critics

Perhaps most crucially for the argument of this book, the rejection of the idea of 'better knowledge' means that the only basis of authority over pupils which such a theory of the curriculum leaves teachers is that of a relationship of unequal power; no wonder this induced a 'fear of knowledge' among some teachers. Bringing knowledge back in[8] to how we think about the curriculum, *as an entitlement*

---

[7]See the reference to Rob Moore and Johan Muller's paper in further readings in Appendix 1.
[8]The title of my 2008 book – see further readings in Appendix 1.

and not necessarily as *a form of domination* takes us to a quite new set of questions concerned with how knowledge is best structured in curricula if such an 'entitlement to knowledge' is to be realized for all pupils. Here, I will mention two important questions about the structuring of knowledge in curricula. The first concerns the boundaries that characterize school knowledge, or to put it another way – what should distinguish curricular from everyday knowledge? Drawing on the ideas of the English sociologist, Basil Bernstein, it is useful to distinguish between two kinds of boundary: those between different fields of knowledge that are represented in the curriculum by the different school subjects, and those between the subject-based knowledge of the curriculum and the everyday knowledge that pupils bring to school. Both types of boundary have their origins in the specialization of educational institutions that has early historical roots but developed fast from the nineteenth century. More recently both types of boundary have been challenged as out of date, backward looking and even elitist. However, although these boundaries are not fixed (they change as new knowledge and new ways of teaching are developed), they do provide a stability for teachers and for pupils in developing their knowledge. Chapter 4 explores the role of subject boundaries as resources for teachers and pupils.

The second and related idea about boundaries is that the curriculum is not only different from our everyday knowledge, but different in a particular way; it is specialized knowledge. In other words, it draws on knowledge that has been developed by researchers investigating different aspects of the world and our experience – the natural world and social worlds as well as the different ways human beings express themselves through such activities such as acting, music, painting and dance and writing. It is knowing how these different types of specialized knowledge are best selected, paced and sequenced for students at different stages of their education, that is the teachers' professional knowledge of the curriculum. Post-apartheid South Africa rightly rejected the rigidities of the previous curriculum. However, their initial critique of apartheid left them with no alternative – with their experience of apartheid, many tended to see any curriculum that specified an entitlement to knowledge as inherently dominating and oppressive. It was this impasse which South Africa is slowly escaping from that led me to recognize the importance of an alternative view of the curriculum that places knowledge as its starting point.

An alternative: The Three Futures approach to the curriculum

In two papers (one with my South African colleague Johan Muller in 2010) and one in 2011 (see further readings in Appendix 1), I began to think about different curriculum models in terms of the approach they take to knowledge. In the 2010 paper, we distinguished three models, which we called Future 1, Future 2 and Future 3 and used them to think about where the present curriculum had come from and what it might be like in the future.

Future 1 referred to the curriculum that secondary schools have inherited from the nineteenth century and was the model that many teachers reacted against since the 1970s, especially those teaching slow or disadvantaged learners. Future 1 was (and is) symbolized by the typical curriculum of grammar and public schools; it formed the basis of the first National Curriculum launched in 1988. Crudely expressed, in Future 1 knowledge is treated as largely given, and established by tradition and by the route it offers high achievers to our leading universities. It tends, although there are differences in practice, to be associated with one-way transmission pedagogy and a view of learning that expects compliance from pupils. For a Future 1 curriculum, the future, despite incremental changes in knowledge, is seen as an extended version of the past.

The first National Curriculum in 1988 was based broadly on Future 1 and presented it as a curriculum for all. However, it was substantially modified in response to complaints from teachers that it lacked flexibility. One consequence has been that the compulsory element of the curriculum up to the age of 16 has been progressively reduced to maths, English and science. This led to a differentiated model of the whole curriculum. A version of Future 1 was maintained for the 'higher achievers' and a more flexible Future 2 model, no longer tied to a broad range of subjects, was developed for the rest. The present Coalition government's reforms can be understood, rhetorically at least, as a return to Future 1 as, at least in principle, a 'Curriculum for all'.

The emergence of a Future 2 curriculum

As secondary education expanded from the 1960s, the school leaving age was raised and increasing numbers of pupils stayed on after the age of 16; the rigidity of the Future 1 gave way under the broad pressure of democratic forces, at least outside the grammar and public schools. Knowledge was no longer treated as given and not open to change but seen as 'constructed' in response to particular needs and interests. At the same time Future 1 became extended as more and more subjects, especially in the social sciences, were included and classics became a minority option rather than holding a position of cultural dominance. In the comprehensive schools a new model, Future 2 emerged, largely for low achievers. Curriculum boundaries between subjects were weakened, as new forms of interdisciplinary studies were introduced and the insulation of school from everyday knowledge became weakened as the curriculum became open to leisure, sports and other community interests.

Future 2 changes were introduced as part of policies of social inclusion and widening participation and were designed to respond to (or cope with) the expanding group of students staying on at school but reluctant to engage with traditional academic subjects. A related trend was the weakening of boundaries between the worlds of school and work as the curriculum was progressively 'vocationalized' for those slower learners who stayed on at school; inevitably, albeit not intentionally, these were pupils from poor and disadvantaged backgrounds.

All these developments represented a change in the old assumptions about knowledge as given and the curriculum as a fixed body of knowledge to be transmitted to all students capable of acquiring it. They represented a change from seeing education as 'worthwhile in itself' (and the phrase barely used today of encouraging 'learning for its own sake') towards an increasingly instrumental view that education was a means to an end – usually expressed as the expectation of future employment. Even the academic curriculum took on these 'instrumental' features. Physics and history were given more priority because they were subjects valued by the top universities, rather than because they involved 'the pursuit of knowledge for its own sake'. These were shifts in the dominant view of curriculum knowledge from something that changed little – even school science below A level barely touched twentieth-century discoveries – to something that could always be changed to suit a new need or interest. This 'socially constructed' view of knowledge was what we referred as underpinning Future 2 developments. For teachers, Future 2 had a number of attractions. First, it was a response to what was perceived as the rigidities and elitism of Future 1. Secondly, if all knowledge were 'socially constructed' and not fixed or given, it licensed a differentiated curriculum as a way of spreading access to all pupils. Whereas programmes preparing older students for university entrance still emphasized traditional subjects, schools were encouraged to develop programmes which emphasized quite different priorities, if they appeared to relate to interests expressed by other pupils.

Despite the majority of pupils attending a comprehensive school by the 1980s, the curriculum of most comprehensive schools was anything but common or comprehensive. Most secondary school teachers graduating from university no doubt still hoped to introduce their pupils to 'the best of what has been thought and said' in their field or subject as I suggested in Chapter 1. However, such ideals faced resistance from reluctant (and therefore failing) pupils and, of no less significance, at least tacit support from the siren voices of some radical educationists. The more extreme versions of such theories dismissed any idea of 'better knowledge' or a 'higher culture' as the right of all pupils.

As a sophisticated, albeit misguided theory of knowledge and culture, the 'social constructivism' that underpinned Future 2 has continued to prove attractive to many teachers and teacher educators. It easily legitimates a curriculum that celebrates the experience of pupils, whatever that may be rather than the idea that the purpose of schools is to introduce them to knowledge beyond their experience.

Back to Future 1?

It is not surprising that for some any reference to the distinctiveness of knowledge is interpreted as elitist and even repressive. The latter years of the Blair and Brown labour governments was characterized by two very different developments which took completely opposite views in the argument that 'knowledge' in any objective sense was indeed elitist. The first was a shift in the government's educational thinking away from subjects and knowledge towards an emphasis on learning as an activity and what became known as twenty-first-century skills or competences such as critical thinking, learning to learn and working with others. The assumption was that with new knowledge being produced more quickly, young people no longer needed to acquire knowledge but to learn how to 'manage' it. There was very little debate or research about such claims; educational research had other priorities, such as depicting the new policies as representing the educational consequences of neo-liberal capitalism. The second development presented a radical alternative to Future 2 and its dominant 'anything goes' approach to knowledge. It was partly tapping a barely articulated unease that young people, even those successful in achieving high grades, were leaving school with little real knowledge to face an increasingly complex world. What is perhaps surprising was that the alternative looked backward not forward. Nor did it emerge from the Left, the education faculties or the teacher unions, the traditional sources of innovative ideas. This second development emerged from Civitas, Reform and Politiea, Right wing Think Thanks completely separate from the wider education community but all linked closely to the Conservative Party. It was as if the long forgotten voice of Rhodes Boyson and the 1970's Black Papers had been reawakened. The new right thinkers were convinced that the curriculum had been 'dumbed down'. However, instead of locating its causes in the policies of previous governments – both Conservative and Labour – young people were seen as the scapegoat and by implication their teachers and, more savagely, the teacher educators. As an almost ready-made solution, they found the American, E. D. Hirsch's book *Cultural Literacy: What Every American Needs to Know*. It had been published in the United States in the late 1980s but was not widely noticed in England at the time. After the formation of the Coalition government in 2010, it soon became apparent that the Think Tanks became a key resource for the government's curriculum reforms – back to Future 1!

A disillusioned educational and political opposition was too depressed to resist the collapse of almost everything that it might have been thought to have stood for and the new Future 1 was born – the past was to be the future.

Unlike the majority of critics on the Left, this book takes the view that the problem with the government's version of Future 1 is not that it endorses a knowledge-led curriculum, but that its version of knowledge fixed in history (you only have to look at the

English syllabus and the first versions of the proposals for History and design technology). Furthermore it includes no plans for how it could become a 'curriculum for all'. Despite these flaws, in focusing on 'knowledge' and in re-emphasizing the key role of school subjects and their links with university disciplines, the government's reforms open a debate about a curriculum for all that was never previously addressed. However, as the next chapter will go on to argue, Futures 1 and 2 need not be the only alternatives.

3

Powerful knowledge as a curriculum principle

Michael Young

Beyond Futures 1 and 2

In this book we argue that both Futures 1 and 2 views of knowledge are partly right but fundamentally mistaken. Of course knowledge is not given as Future 1 assumes; it has social and historical origins as Future 2 argues. What other origins could it have? However it does not follow as Future 2 assumes that because knowledge is social, there is no 'better knowledge'. Newton and Shakespeare are historical figures who made discoveries and wrote plays in their contexts which were very different from ours. But we still go to Shakespeare's plays, and recognize that although they are about a society that we only dimly know about through history books, their characters and relationships articulate for us almost universal truths. Likewise, we find that for human beings living on this planet, Newton's laws of motion and light are as near the truth as we can get – today, as they were in the 1970s, and before he discovered them in the late 1600s. So being social and historical doesn't just (as of course it can) make knowledge biased, it also makes it true. Why? Because what is true, is not just 'in the knowledge defined as a set of propositions' – as in the dominant philosophical argument about knowledge being 'justified true belief'. Newton's laws, to take but one example, locate their claim to be true in the community of physicists[1] who have, since his time, tested and questioned them. Whether these specialist communities are particle physicists, novelists or social scientists, such communities have their shared rules, some more and some less agreed than others, for testing and questioning the truth of whatever they claim to know in their field. The truth, and the objectivity of knowledge is the truth of these communities, as the nearest to truth that we get – that is the truth of Future 3. These communities, some more open and some more fragmented than others, are the specialist disciplinary communities largely located in universities, and in the increasingly global communities of which university researchers are a part. The subjects of a Future 3 curriculum are both supported and challenged by the discoveries of the members of the disciplinary communities that they are associated with and by the research undertaken by the associations of subject teachers with their expertise in how different children learn and what are the best activities that will encourage them to take their learning further. The issue of subjects is considered specifically in Chapters 4 and 7 which takes geography as a case study.

---

[1]It is only in the past hundred years that they have been known as physicists and not a branch of natural philosophy.

What is Future 3?

On the one hand, Future 3 points to a curriculum of the future and so offers a vision of the future for schools today. On the other hand, it is an element of all actual curricula which are under the conflicting pressures to lean towards Future 1 (the public and other elite schools) and Future 2 (comprehensive schools with significant proportion of disadvantaged pupils). It differs in its idea of knowledge from Futures 1 and 2 in a number of ways. In contrast to Future 1, it explicitly locates knowledge in the specialist communities of researchers in different fields and as a consequence, does not treat knowledge as 'given' but fallible and always open to change through the debates and research of the particular specialist community. Unlike the openness of knowledge assumed by Future 2, the openness of Future 3 is not arbitrary or responsive to any kind of challenge; it is bounded by the epistemic rules of the particular specialist communities. It follows that a Future 3 curriculum rejects *the a-social givenness* of school subjects associated with Future 1 and the scepticism about subject knowledge associated with Future 2. Instead it treats *subjects* as the most reliable tools we have for enabling students to acquire knowledge and make sense of the world. In other words, a Future 3 curriculum is a resource for teachers who seek to take their students beyond their experience in the most reliable ways we have. It implies that the curriculum must stipulate the concepts associated with different subjects and how they are related, whether they refer to energy, matter, literature or historical change. It is the systematic interrelatedness of subject-based concepts and how they take their meaning from how they relate to each other that distinguishes them from the everyday concepts of experience that pupils bring to school, which always relate to specific contexts and experiences. Concepts, however, must be linked to the contents or facts that give them meaning and to the activities involved in acquiring them. It is the link between concepts, contents and activities that distinguishes a Future 3 curriculum from Hirsch's lists of 'what every child should know'. It points to a new and always changing balance between the *stability of subject concepts* (implicit and overemphasized in Future 1 and underemphasized in Future 2), *changes in content* (underemphasized in Future 1) as new knowledge is produced and *the activities involved in learning* (overemphasized in Future 2). The three Futures is not a new curriculum model waiting to be 'implemented' by schools. The three Futures model offers *a way of thinking* about the most important issue a curriculum leader ever faces – the question of knowledge. Elements of Future 3, and of course Futures 1 and 2, are not new and are to be found to varying degrees in every subject and in the curriculum of every school.

In order to try and specify what the idea of a Future 3 curriculum might involve, I have been developing with colleagues, the idea of 'powerful knowledge' as a curriculum principle. As an idea it needs much further development and is only outlined here. It has been picked up by some involved in teacher education and by specialists in history (see the Chapter 5 by Martin Roberts and the work by Christine Counsell at Cambridge) and geography teaching (Chapter 7 in this book by David Lambert). It aims to be a conceptual resource relevant both to a school's whole curriculum policy as is illustrated by Carolyn Roberts (Chapter 6) and her 'knowledge-led school' as well as across the range of subjects. The next section describes the idea of powerful knowledge in more detail, pointing out some of its possibilities and pitfalls.

Powerful knowledge and the role of headteachers

Underlying the arguments of this chapter is the view that our education system, and every school in it like any other, faces two basic but related issues. The first issue is how far can a school reach a shared understanding about the knowledge they want their pupils to acquire and on what basis is such an agreement to be reached. In most countries on the European continent, there is wide agreement at a national level on both issues and politicians rarely intervene; this makes the professional work of teachers more straightforward and on the whole the school systems of such countries are more successful than ours. In a country like England, where there is less far agreement (except within the small (7%) section of schools which rely on parents' fees), politicians, at least after the 1960s, have been unable to resist intervening in what was once called the 'secret garden' of the curriculum. This intervention into state-funded institutions is understandable in a democracy; however, too much political intervention, of any kind, undermines the sources of autonomy of teaching, which, like any profession, depends on specialist knowledge.

The second issue will be more familiar to readers. If a school can broadly agree on what the knowledge is that all pupils are entitled to, how does it ensure that as high a proportion as possible of each cohort of students have access to that knowledge. This is essentially a pedagogic issue shaped by decisions made about the curriculum. Such issues face every school but there will be far easier answers for some schools than others. It is worth therefore, for the sake of illustration, describing two very different hypothetical cases. There are schools – usually but not always grammar or 'public' schools, in which the vast majority of pupils achieve almost 100 per cent grade 'A's at GCSE and the majority of their students gain 'A's or 'B's at A level. In such schools, both the curriculum and the pedagogic questions have less urgency. This does not, of course, mean that such questions do not need to be asked. Some university admission tutors have recently commented that students from elite schools, even those with 'A's and 'A*' grades, find difficulty in thinking critically. This suggests that, for understandable reasons, schools place 'teaching to the test', even for high achievers, above the broader educational purpose of 'teaching for understanding'. However, for those schools which find achieving the national average or above for the proportion of pupils achieving 5 GCSEs at grades A*–C (even according to the pre-EBacc measures) is beyond them, answers to these questions will be different and far more challenging. It is such schools that have in the past been led to develop a more differentiated post-14 curriculum. With the changes initiated by the present government in the regulations governing the equivalence of different certificates for GCSE, this option is likely to be less available. However, the issue that arises from the concept of 'powerful knowledge' is broader and goes beyond the scope of individual schools. It starts from the idea of citizens being equal before the law and extending that to the idea that children as future citizens all have the same educational rights. The National Curriculum (and each school curriculum) should therefore be a guarantee of those rights. It follows that the curriculum of every school represents the entitlement to knowledge for *all* the children at that school. In other words, a school curriculum (and indeed the national curriculum) should not discriminate in curriculum terms between children on grounds of ethnicity, gender, family circumstances or assumed ability or motivation. The curriculum can in this sense be seen as a guarantor of equality – at least equality of opportunity – and it must be stipulated independently of the social composition of pupils attending a particular school. To fulfil this requirement this book argues that the curriculum must be based on the 'best knowledge we have' or be a clear set of stages towards that 'best knowledge'. That is the premise of the idea of 'powerful knowledge' and why a skill-based curriculum that focuses on functional literacy and numeracy skills can never be the basis of a curriculum that claims to be an entitlement to English (both language and literature) or mathematics. Skills have their place in the curriculum but skills on their own limit the student to tackling 'how' questions and not 'what' questions. It is only 'what' questions that take students beyond their experience and enable them to engage with and grasp alternatives. The next section presents a short introduction to the origins of the concept 'powerful knowledge'.

Whether one interprets the recent reforms as limiting autonomy, or greater freedom, the head's role as a curriculum leader is crucial. I want to propose the concept of 'powerful knowledge' as a resource for heads in their curriculum leadership role, as a basis for an agreement in their school on 'what it should teach' as well as for achieving greater equality of outcomes and a more socially just society.

'Powerful knowledge' and 'knowledge of the powerful'

Although linking the two words 'power' and 'knowledge' is neither new nor specific to education, the concept of 'powerful knowledge' as an educational idea distinguishing types of knowledge does appear to be relatively new; it has become part of curriculum debates within the past five years. I did not start with 'powerful knowledge' as a separate term to distinguish types of knowledge. Initially I found it helpful to link it to the similar term that reverses the words, knowledge and power as expressed in the term 'knowledge of the powerful'. However, as I will explain, the two terms 'powerful knowledge' and 'knowledge of the powerful' use the word 'power' and, as a consequence, the word 'knowledge' in very different ways.

I first used the couple of terms to distinguish two different ways of linking power and knowledge when thinking about the curriculum. Simply, put, 'knowledge of the powerful' focuses on those people or groups with power in any society or organization to define what knowledge is. In the case of the school curriculum, the concept 'knowledge of the powerful' refers to what knowledge is included and what is not and by whom. Karl Marx's version of 'knowledge of the powerful' will be familiar to many readers. It asserts that 'The ideas of the ruling class are in every epoch the ruling ideas.' It became a popular idea in the 1970s among educationalists on the Left for several reasons. First, it focused on the question 'who benefits from existing definitions and selections of knowledge?' Secondly, and specifically in relation to the curriculum, it focuses on the question 'who has the power to exclude and include certain topic and concepts in the curriculum?' The questions it raised were concerned with the interests expressed when some knowledge is excluded or included in the curriculum. A good example from the nineteenth century was the exclusion of geology from the school curriculum on the grounds that it might undermine students' belief in the version of creation found in the first book of Genesis. This was not an example of either an epistemological or an educational reason. Thirdly, in relation to education policy, the idea of 'knowledge of the powerful' was a way of shifting the blame for why so many pupils failed in school – from the pupils, their teachers and their families – to the curriculum and thus to those who controlled it. If the curriculum is understood as a product of the interests of those with power, and it is argued that it is the curriculum which causes the failure of working-class pupils and makes them feel inferior, we must blame 'the powerful' and not the pupils themselves for not working hard enough or their teachers for not developing a more effective or appropriate pedagogy.

The problem with such an approach is that like the broader idea of knowledge being 'socially constructed' that I discussed as underpinning Future 2 in Chapter 1, it tells us very little about the curriculum or what alternatives to the existing curriculum might be possible. The curriculum from this perspective is always primarily a political instrument not an educational instrument to support learning. The idea contains an element of truth and is challenging to curriculum policy makers and to curriculum leaders in schools, but in practice, is of very little help to either. As the late Basil Bernstein once wrote, 'education cannot compensate for society'. In other words, the roots of inequality are in the society not in the curriculum; at the same time it is important to ask what the curriculum can do for pupils that make it worthwhile, even if we cannot expect it to 'compensate for society'. It is in addressing that question that I was led to the concept of 'powerful knowledge'.

In contrast to the idea of the curriculum as 'knowledge of the powerful', the idea of 'powerful knowledge' refers to features of the particular knowledge itself that is included in the curriculum and what it can do for those who have access to it. The concept of powerful knowledge is not concerned with the distribution of power, at least not directly. Another way of putting it is that powerful knowledge refers to the knowledge not the knowers. It is not concerned with who defines or creates the knowledge. Knowledge is 'powerful' if it predicts, if it explains, if it enables you to envisage alternatives.

If then these are some of the 'powers' of powerful knowledge, how might we distinguish it from knowledge that does not offer the potential knower any specific intellectual resources? I will suggest three criteria for defining *powerful knowledge* that may be useful for heads and their staff in evaluating their curriculum and which bring together some of the ideas discussed earlier in this chapter:

- *It is distinct from the 'common-sense' knowledge we acquire through our everyday experience.*
  Common-sense knowledge is not only vital in our everyday lives but it is also always tied to particular contexts; if we live in city X we acquire much local knowledge of that city; however this tells us nothing about city Y or cities in general. Our common-sense knowledge develops through experience as we grow older; it does not need teaching and we do not need to go to school to acquire it. However, it is

limited because it is tied to the contexts of our experience
and it is to overcome these limitations that we have schools.

- *It is systematic* – its concepts are *systematically related to each other* in groups that we refer to as subjects or disciplines.
  It is not like common sense rooted in the specific contexts
  of our experience. This means that 'powerful knowledge'
  can be the basis for generalizations and thinking beyond
  particular contexts or cases. The clearest examples of both
  the systematic structure of powerful knowledge and that it
  is a resource for generalizing are found in the mathematical
  and physical sciences. However, other forms of knowledge
  such as the social sciences, humanities and the arts also have
  concepts that take us beyond particular cases and contexts
  in different ways and offer some, albeit more limited and
  different (because of the nature of the phenomena they are
  concerned with) capacities for generalization.

- *It is specialized.*
  In other words powerful knowledge is knowledge that
  has been developed by clearly distinguishable groups,
  usually occupations, with a clearly defined focus or field
  of enquiry and relatively fixed boundaries separating their
  form of expertise from other forms. These groups range
  from novelists and playwrights to nuclear physicists and
  marketing specialists. The specialist character of powerful
  knowledge explains, at least in part, why it is experienced
  as difficult to acquire and why acquiring it requires
  specialist teachers.

Powerful knowledge and curriculum specialization

In universities this *specialization of knowledge* takes the form of disciplines separated by boundaries and directed to discovering or developing new knowledge. Even those who work in interdisciplinary research fields like town planning and transport draw on disciplines and collaborate with those from different disciplines until, in some cases, a new discipline is established with shared rules of enquiry (examples are biochemistry and cultural history). There are debates both about how far it is useful to think of some disciplines being foundational for more applied fields – in both the pedagogic sense (some should be taught before others) and the epistemological sense (some disciplines be 'reduced' to others).

In schools this specialization has a number of aspects. First, the dominant model is subject- not discipline-based. Secondly, subjects are drawn from disciplines – a useful concept to describe how this happens is 'recontextualization'. Whereas disciplines are primarily oriented to the discovery of new knowledge (the production of new knowledge) subjects are oriented to the transmission of knowledge (the reproduction of knowledge for the next generation) and have to take account of the stage of development of learners in how knowledge content is selected (from disciplines), paced and sequenced, as well as relevance of the different theories of learning and other factors that may influence student progress.

The important curriculum point about subjects is that, like disciplines, they are specialized forms of knowledge based on the shared rules of subject communities within which their questions, methods, concepts and criteria are debated and discussed. Subjects should not be seen as fixed but that does not mean they cannot support the acquisition of 'powerful knowledge' as is discussed in Chapter 2. The other point about specialization which is beyond the scope of this book is that in all schools specialization separates students after the age of 16 into programmes bringing together different subjects in different ways. The distribution of post-16 students is a product of decisions by those teaching these students and the students' choice. The options that are made available and the different groupings of subjects is a crucial part of the curriculum planning of a school. The most familiar form of specialization for post-16 students is that between curricula based on groups of academic subjects and curricula oriented to particular occupational sectors such as health or engineering.

Powerful knowledge and cultural values

The criteria of powerful knowledge refer to the *structure* of a form of knowledge (how it is organized) and its *function* (what it is for). Insofar as they embody values, these criteria are the broad values of objectivity, openness to debate, reason, logic and respect for all human beings. Criteria for powerful knowledge are concerned with truth; they are not ways of valuing different cultures or beliefs. This distinction between truth and value puts a responsibility on teachers to distinguish between respecting the values that their pupils bring to school as representing the culture they come from, and challenging the validity of their explanations in relation to the criteria of different subjects such as history or biology. To take an example, a biology teacher must tell her or his pupils about the arguments and evidence for the theory of evolution are the nearest to the truth that we have about how life has developed; at the same time she or he must respect religious *beliefs* that some students may hold (e.g. that 'the world was created by God in six days'). Another example I came across when I was in New Zealand was that in fishing communities, Maori children are brought up to believe that 2 + 2 = 3, not 4 as in Western (or universal) maths; the explanation of this is that in some Maori communities fishermen are always expected to return one fish in every four they catch in order to preserve the stock of fish. The curriculum problem is in distinguishing the universal truths of mathematics as it underpins the professional role of the maths teacher and the culture values of the Maori community.

The principle underlying the idea of 'powerful knowledge' is that in any curriculum field there is 'better' knowledge. However, 'better' has a different meaning in different fields. Some specialist fields – to varying degrees in the social sciences, the humanities and the arts – are characterized by sharp disagreements within the specialist communities. In such cases the responsibility of the teacher is to make her or his students aware of these differences and as far as possible, what their bases are and why such arguments matter.

The concept of powerful knowledge: Some implications for schools

Each school will develop their curriculum based on the National Curriculum in their own way. What the idea of 'powerful knowledge' does is to provide a framework for thinking about the decisions that they have to make. For example:

- What subjects does a school offer and what choices are offered to students at different ages?

- Does a school think such general themes such as citizenship, the environment and personal and health education are important?

- If so, does this mean that the curriculum or part of it can be organized on the basis of such themes, or should it be the responsibility of different specialist subjects?

- In what sense do subjects like business administration, communications and environmental science give students access to 'powerful knowledge' that enables them to progress to higher levels? What is the powerful knowledge that is implicit in such subjects? Can it be made explicit?

- Do the vocational and community-oriented courses that may be offered by a school comply with the criteria of 'powerful knowledge', if so how and if not what are the criteria for including them in the curriculum?

- How do the criteria of 'powerful knowledge' apply in different ways to the sciences, humanities, arts and explicitly vocational subjects?

As with any idea that aims to make sense of complex practical situations and decisions, the idea of 'powerful knowledge' needs to be explored and tried out in a range of contexts across a range of subjects. This could hopefully be the basis for a dialogue between teachers and curriculum theorists which would lead to some revision, clarification and greater specification of what ideas like 'differentiated from experience', 'specialized' and 'being systematic' mean for different subjects and across the curriculum as a whole. This would either lead to new concepts or to better definitions. Such dialogues have already begun to take place with history and geography specialists. It is important that they are extended across the whole range of subjects and include 'vocational' and applied subjects as well as the more traditional sciences and humanities. We should not prejudge the extent to which vocational or applied subjects offer (or fail to offer) students access to powerful knowledge. Such discussions are also necessary to help clarify a number of issues barely touched on in this chapter. For example, what vision of education of the whole person is implied by a curriculum based on powerful knowledge? How far does it take us beyond the traditional subject-based curriculum I described earlier as Future 1? In what sense does Future 3 offer a modern forward looking interpretation of 'general education' or 'liberal education for all'?

Finally we need to give more precise attention to the relationships between curriculum and pedagogy and between a National and a school curriculum that I argued for in Chapter 2 as well as how these relationships connect to the rethinking of the relationship between assessment, pedagogy and curriculum that I touched on at the beginning of this chapter.

Powerful knowledge and alternatives as principles of curricular justice

If the idea of 'powerful knowledge' became widely adopted as the basis for the curriculum in English secondary schools it would be a change with even bigger implications than the decision in many local authorities in 1965 to give up the 11+ examination and reorganize secondary education along comprehensive lines. It would in effect be saying that at least up to 16, there would be a common curriculum based on common principles for *all* pupils. This would mean reassessing all current pre-16 programmes according to the criteria for powerful knowledge and would lead to the removal or transformation of some existing programmes from a school's curriculum. It could be a central decision from the Department of Education as has been a feature of many of the recent changes. Alternatively it could follow the relatively autonomous decisions of individual schools. Whether the government-led or school-led approach was adopted there would undoubtedly be resistance from some schools and from within some schools. It is therefore worth considering the arguments for and against the idea of powerful knowledge and opposition to it.

A knowledge-led curriculum of the kind this book is proposing starts from two principles which have up to now been seen in conflict by the majority of educationists. The first, as already discussed – is that 'powerful knowledge' – is the knowledge that pupils have a right of access to that defines their entitlement as pupils. Furthermore, this knowledge has its own rules and criteria which judge all pupils equally, apart from the severely mentally handicapped. That is the starting point for an equal, fair and just system; it is fair and just because it is based on the most reliable criteria of 'best knowledge' that we have and is the same for all pupils. Such a curriculum principle takes no account of any differences in perceived or measured ability, disposition, motivation, interest or prior experience of pupils. Currently, the curriculum of most schools (and the National Curriculum) is not differentiated until pupils are 14 (the end of Key Stage 3). From that age most schools begin to identify different abilities, motivations and interests and how they are distributed among each cohort of pupils. The two overriding factors likely to influence decisions about a student's further curriculum have no relationship to powerful knowledge criteria – they are likely to be individual choice and evidence of past attainment. They have no connection at all with 'powerful knowledge' criteria where the sole aim is to further the student's intellectual development in different fields. We can assume that these decisions are made on the basis of what the school thinks are the best interests of the pupils. The question which this raises, which is far from new but has all too easily been avoided: by taking the different interests, motivations and abilities of students into account, and modifying the criteria from those of "powerful knowledge", do such curricular decisions still represent the principles of treating all students equally? It could be argued that by excluding some students from access to powerful knowledge on the basis of their choice and prior attainment, that such differentiated curricula do not comply with the principle of equality for all pupils at least up to the age of 16.

Our argument on the issues of equality and social justice is that by excluding some students from the opportunity to acquire 'powerful knowledge' on the basis of their choice and prior attainment, differentiated curricula do not follow the principle of *entitlement to knowledge for all pupils* at least up to the age of 16. This does not mean of course that what follows from such a principle is easy or straightforward for schools or that suddenly 'academic failures' are turned into even modest 'successes'. What it does is to set an agenda for pedagogic and curricula innovation at a school level; it could also be the basis for putting political pressure on governments for more resources. It is worth returning to the idea of a 'differentiated curriculum' that was considered historically in earlier chapters, in a little more detail. Not only is it the twenty-first-century residue of the Future 2 approach that began to emerge in the 1970s, but also it represents what might be called the mainstream Educational Left alternative to Michael Gove's Future 1. This also may make clearer that we are not closet supporters of Gove and his policies, but are also proposing an alternative to the mainstream Left. Supporters of a differentiated secondary school curriculum often treat the claim made in this book that a knowledge-based curriculum is objectively a 'better' curriculum for *all students* as little more than prejudice and class snobbery which can only disadvantage those assumed to be 'non-academic'. Their argument goes that community-oriented programmes like the RSA's 'Open Minds' curriculum discussed earlier treats such students differently because they have different needs which a subject-based knowledge-led curriculum does not take account of. In this book we propose a very different approach to the curriculum that starts not with different types of children, but that many children are excluded from what schools can offer and from their entitlement. All children, we argue, are entitled to a foundation of 'powerful knowledge' up to the age of 16. It is only on the basis of such knowledge, that they are likely to be able to make the best choices that will decide their educational future. Access to knowledge is what the struggle for schooling since the nineteenth century has been about, and, since the 1960s, what the movement for comprehensive schools has been about. There is no good argument for comprehensive secondary schools if they are not based on a common curriculum. As teachers we must value some types of education more than others, even if this may have similarities to the curriculum of elite schools or aspects of Michael Gove's 2014 National Curriculum proposals. It is absurd to imagine that the rich will not purchase the best education available, just as they buy the best surgeons; the inequality is in the distribution of opportunities, not the surgery – or the education. This poses difficult problems for those on the Left. If we are serious about educational equality we have to be serious about curricular justice, and for all its limitations Gove's EBacc points to the idea of entitlement to knowledge more clearly than anything proposed before. All children have a right to study a foreign language, at least one humanities subject, and at least one science as well as English and maths; it is hard to disagree with this as an entitlement up to the age of 16.

We have no time for Gove's traditional, old-fashioned and backward-looking view of knowledge which in this book we criticize as returning to Future 1. However unless there is no such thing as 'better' or more objective knowledge, his emphasis on knowledge is right. If there is 'better knowledge' then surely access to it is everyone's right. Denying that access to some in the name of diversity, however linked to a concern for the welfare of the students concerned, is not about promoting equality or social justice. Some children will succeed in life as a result of any curriculum (or even none). However if you find yourself on a course that includes numeracy or mathematical literacy and not mathematics, it may not matter if you hope to be a professional footballer or a fashion model or a hair dresser, but it will make it very difficult for you to go on to be an engineer. Likewise, if you want to start your own business you will need some systematic knowledge of accounting. This is not prejudice on the part of the engineering and business communities; it is because there is such a thing as mathematical truth that is important for engineers and anyone running their own business.

Differentiating the curriculum based on a respect for cultural and individual differences becomes, in effect, a support for inequality. Many school curricula do not start from the premise of 'powerful knowledge *for all pupils*'. As a result, those who find learning difficult in the early years of secondary school[2] are often offered easier and more 'interesting' courses misleadingly labelled 'vocational'. This may solve an immediate problem for the school but in doing so it denies access to the knowledge that they will need as adults to those pupils taking these easier courses. Perhaps the most troubling thing about those who dismiss a knowledge-based curriculum and equate it with Gove's proposals is that although they are invariably graduates in positions of authority in society, and often have children

---

[2]This may well be the result of inadequate preparation in the primary school.

who are graduates, they only ever seem to think about the children of people who are not like themselves. Would they ever conceive of allowing their children to take a Level 2 diploma in leisure and tourism? Not all ways of learning or all curricula are as good as each other. It is not the qualification title that is the issue or whether it is academic or vocational; it is the knowledge it provides access to. For example, Leisure and Tourism diplomas include one or two foreign languages and economics in similar programmes in some other European countries. One example that illustrates this point always haunts me. A friend of my daughter's who got a string of 'A's and 'B's at GCSE was also an enthusiastic cook. So he decided to take a catering diploma instead of A levels. He lasted no more than six weeks, bored at how little he was required to learn. It was as if the lecturers had never had student with good GCSEs on their course before and assumed that it was for those with low grades and a reluctant attitude to learning. I mention this not to generalize from one example, but to highlight that the issue is access to knowledge, not the label given to different courses.

A curriculum based on the idea of 'powerful knowledge' does not of itself promote social justice or solve the problem of low achievement and inequality; some pupils will continue to fail or achieve little. In practical terms this calls on any school facing persistent low achievement to think again about possible alternatives for its slow learners and the possibilities of extra coaching, additional staff development and extended programmes that take slower learners longer but do not lead to courses which will leave them at a disadvantage in their future lives. This is not of course to say that low achievement can always be overcome within the school; it is also and fundamentally a resource issue. It does however provide a starting point for a serious debate about educational equality and what this means. Although such a curriculum leaves unresolved the broader issues of inequality and social injustice, it focuses explicitly on what a school can do and the limits of what it can do. The alternative that follows from rejecting the idea of powerful knowledge has never been more starkly expressed than recently by Raewyn Connell (2012), the distinguished Australian sociologist. Her definition of curricular justice is:

> a curriculum organized around the experience, culture and needs of the least advantaged members of the society – rather than the most advantaged, as things stand now. A socially just curriculum will draw extensively on indigenous knowledge, working class experience, women's experience, immigrant cultures, multiple languages.[3]

This seems, despite its radical edge, to be no more than a prescription for leaving the 'disadvantaged' where they are. The advantage of taking such an extreme statement seriously, even for a moment, is that one is forced to think of alternatives. From the perspective of this book, Connell seems to making a similar mistake to one that is not uncommon among educationalists in this country. She collapses the profoundly important humanist principle of valuing and respecting human experiences in all their diversity with treating these experiences as if they were versions of the best ways we have of making sense of the world. There is no way

---

[3]R. Connell (2012), Just education, *Journal of Education Policy*, 27, 5: 681–3.

that 'powerful knowledge' can be based on the experience of non-indigenous, middle-class, male, monolingual, non-immigrants or in fact, anyone's *experience*.

The argument of our book is precisely the opposite – if education is to be emancipatory, and we know that it is possible for any of the groups listed by Connell, it has to be based on a break with experience. It has been that break that has been the basis of human societies and the source of human progress as Emile Durkheim, the first greatest sociologist of education showed over a century ago. For all the flaws and failures that it led to, it was that break with experience found in the most primitive societies and the knowledge it led to that points to the possibility of greater equality and social justice and is, of course, also the basis of the emancipatory possibilities of schooling.

4

The progressive case for a subject-based curriculum

Michael Young

Introduction

Much is written in current educational policies about preparing students for a knowledge society and the important role education has to play. These policies, however, say very little about the role of knowledge itself in education. What is it, in other words, that is important that our young people know? More worrying than this, many current policies almost systematically neglect or marginalize the question of knowledge. The emphasis is invariably on learners, their different styles of learning and their interests, on measurable learning outcomes and competences and making the curriculum relevant to their experience and their future employability. Knowledge is somehow a taken for granted or something we can make fit our political goals.

It would not, in the case of England, Scotland and some other European countries, be overstating the case, to say that the recent curriculum reforms are leading to a reduction or even an 'evacuation of content', especially for those already not succeeding in school. Often these reforms are well intentioned and have progressive aims. They stress opening access, widening participation and promoting social inclusion. This makes them difficult to question without being seen as conservative and elitist.

In this chapter, I want to make the case that if we are to give the importance of education in a knowledge society any serious meaning, we need to make the question of knowledge our central concern and this involves developing a knowledge-led and subject-led, and not, as much current orthodoxy assumes, a learner-led approach to the curriculum. Furthermore, I will argue that this is the 'radical' option – not as some claim, the 'conservative' option – provided we are clear about what we mean by knowledge. I use the term 'radical' here to refer to the key issue facing most countries today: the persistence of social inequalities in education. I prefer the term 'radical' to alternatives such as 'progressive' and 'critical'. Whereas the former term has had a close, and in my view, unfortunate association with learner-centred pedagogies and the emphasis on 'learning from experience', the latter term, despite being part of a much broader intellectual heritage that can be traced back to Kant and the eighteenth-century Enlightenment, has, in educational studies, been equated with the empty rhetoric of much of what passes for *critical pedagogy*.

The rest of this chapter is concerned with how we think about the curriculum; it has two parts. First, I draw on the example of the 2008 reforms of the National Curriculum in England, which I describe as adopting an 'instrumentalist' approach. I will explain what I mean later by this. I will argue that instead we need to see the curriculum not as an instrument for achieving goals such as 'contributing to the economy' or 'motivating disaffected learners' but as intrinsic to why we have schools at all. The second part of this chapter shifts focus from the curriculum to schools and suggests how school subjects can be thought of as the major resource for the work of teachers and pupils in school.

In the final section, I address two of the strongest arguments made against a subject or, more broadly, against a knowledge-based curriculum. The first argument is that any form of subject-based curriculum will continue to discriminate against disadvantaged, and particularly working class and some ethnic minority pupils. This issue has a particular urgency in the United Kingdom at this time. A traditional subject-based curriculum is strongly endorsed by the new Conservative Secretary of State, Michael Gove. A month before the general election he was quoted as saying that he was an unashamed curriculum traditionalist, and he believed that most parents wanted their children:

> to sit in rows, learn about Kings and Queens, read great works, do proper mental arithmetic, start algebra by 11 and learn foreign languages. (Gove, 2009)

It is important to distinguish between Gove's traditional view of a subject-based curriculum and the view of curriculum that we argue for in this book. I shall do this in two ways: in terms of their different concepts of knowledge, and in terms of the different assumptions they make about learners' relationships to knowledge.

The traditional model treats knowledge as given and as something that students have to comply with. In contrast, although the model I am arguing for also treats knowledge as external to learners, it recognizes that this externality is not given, but has a social and historical basis. I also distinguish the knowledge-based curriculum I am arguing for, from the traditional model by their different relationships with learners and, therefore, their different implications for pedagogy and what teachers and pupils do. The former I shall refer to as a 'curriculum based on compliance' and the latter as a 'curriculum based on engagement'.

What the two models have in common and where they stand in contrast to the instrumentalist model that underpins the 2008 reforms in England is that both start with knowledge and not the learner, nor the contexts faced by learners, as is implied by curricula designed to accommodate learner's future employment prospects.

The second argument against a subject-based curriculum, which I will comment on more briefly at the end, is the claim that it is at odds with what is often claimed to be a global trend towards de-differentiation, in other words, towards the weakening of boundaries between occupations and knowledge domains.

The 2008 reforms in England: Instrumentalist curricula and their problems

Curriculum policies are inevitably developed in social, political and economic contexts. My argument is that in the past decade, under well-known global pressures, curriculum designers in the United Kingdom have taken too much account of these contexts in two senses. First, they have responded to governmental pressure to contribute to solving social problems such as unemployment.

Secondly, they have also responded to what they perceive as learners' needs and interests, especially those learners who achieve little in school or leave early.

As a consequence, the proposals have neglected or at least played down the fundamental educational role of the curriculum, which derives both from what schools are for and what they can and cannot do. While we must remain mindful of the wider context, curriculum choices have to be addressed for what they are: alternative ways of promoting the intellectual development of young people. The more we focus on how a reformed curriculum might solve social or economic problems, the less likely those social and economic problems will be addressed where they originate, which is not in the school.

A former prime minister, Tony Blair once stated, 'education is the best economic policy that we have'. This said much, by implication, about his economic policies. However, it also represents the kind of instrumentalism that has plagued educational policies in England for the past 30 years; it addresses what politicians hope that education can do 'as a means', not what it is for 'as an end'. It is as if questions about the purposes of education are too philosophical and abstract for policy makers and politicians. Philosophers of education tend to focus on very general ideas that schools should promote human well-being. However, although well-being is an important goal for all societies, it is as much a goal for families and communities as schools, and says little about the distinctive role of the curriculum.

The major priorities of the 2008 reforms were to shift the balance away from subject content to topical themes that cut across a range of subjects, and to seek ways of personalizing the curriculum by relating it more directly to pupil's everyday knowledge and experiences. The

curriculum designers began with two genuine problems that I am
sure are not unique to England: an 'overcrowded' curriculum, and
too many disaffected students. The reforms attempted to link the
two in accounting for the failure of schools to motivate a significant
proportion of students. The reformed curriculum put a greater
emphasis on its flexibility and its relevance to the experience that
students bring to school. In other words, they viewed the curriculum
as an instrument for motivating students to learn.

Why is this a problem?

This chapter builds on a short paper by Tim Oates[1] who argues that
an instrumentalist approach to the curriculum both misunderstands
what any curriculum can do, and confuses two crucially separate
educational ideas. The first idea concerns *curriculum*, which refers to
the knowledge that a country agrees is important for all students to
have access to. The second idea concerns *pedagogy*, which, in contrast,
refers to the activities of teachers in motivating students and helping
them to engage with the curriculum and make it meaningful.

Curriculum and pedagogy, I suggest, need to be seen as
conceptually distinct. They refer to the distinct responsibilities of
curriculum designers and teachers and each depends on the other.
Whereas teachers cannot create a curriculum themselves, they need
it to guide them in what they have to teach, curriculum designers
can only stipulate the important concepts that pupils need access to.

---

[1] T. Oates (2009), *Missing the Point: Identifying a Well-Grounded Common Core*,
Cambridge: Cambridge Assessment.

Curriculum designers rely on teachers to motivate students and give those concepts a reality for pupils.

Attempts to include the experiences of students in a 'more motivational' curriculum blur the curriculum/pedagogy distinction and the very different roles of curriculum designers and teachers. As most teachers know well, they have to take account of the experiences and prior knowledge that students bring to school and what initially motivates them. These are part of the resources teachers have for mobilizing students and are the basis for students to become active learners. That is quite different, however, from including these experiences in the curriculum.

I want to mention two other problems that can arise from an instrumentalist view of the curriculum. Both are related to the blurring of the distinction between curriculum and pedagogy and hence both lead directly to a discussion of the role that subjects have in the curriculum. First, an instrumentalist view of curriculum *can* lead to the proliferation of specific guidelines for teachers.[2] Although teachers are not statutorily required to adopt these guidelines, the authoritative nature of their origins in the QCDA,[3] together with their links to subject specifications on which examinations are based, made them difficult to ignore. The assumption of the guidelines appears to be that a solution to the lack of motivation of students is more curriculum guidance for teachers rather than strengthening and supporting their subject and pedagogic knowledge, and as a consequence, their professionalism.

---

[2] www.qcda.gov.uk/curriculum/36.aspx
[3] Qualifications and Curriculum Development Authority in England since abolished by the Coalition government in 2011.

In a wider political context where much stress is laid on pupil grades and test scores and where schools can be ranked nationally on the numbers gaining certificates, it is not stretching the argument too far to suggest that the curriculum itself is increasingly becoming a form of accountability rather than a guide for teachers. Two contrasting examples of curriculum specifications illustrate this point. One came from the QCDA and was being used by a state school; it was 10–12 pages long. The other, from an examination board, was being used by a fee-paying private (in English terms, public) school and was a page and a half long. Both addressed the issue of quality. However, they had very different ideas of teacher professionalism, the distinction between curriculum and pedagogy, and how far teachers could be trusted.

The second problem that arises from treating the curriculum as an 'instrument' is that it becomes possible for governments to claim that social or economic problems can be 'solved' by changes in the curriculum. I am not denying that the curriculum should always be open to democratic debate. However, unless political demands from governments have to face explicit educational criteria from curriculum designers about what a curriculum can do, there is a danger that the more fundamental purposes of schooling, to take pupils beyond their experience in ways that they would be unlikely to have access to at home, will be neglected. That surely is what schools are for.

To summarize my argument so far: first, the curriculum needs to be seen as having a purpose of its own: the intellectual development of students. It should not be treated as a means for motivating students or for solving social problems. Secondly, intellectual development is a concept-based not a content-based or skill-based process. This means that the curriculum should be concept-based. However, concepts are always about something. They imply some contents and not others. Content, therefore, is important, not as facts to be memorized, as in the old curriculum, but because without it students cannot acquire concepts and, therefore, will not develop their understanding and progress in their learning. Thirdly, it is important to distinguish curriculum and pedagogy as they relate differently to school knowledge and the everyday knowledge pupils bring to school in different ways. The curriculum should exclude the everyday knowledge of students, whereas that knowledge is a resource for the pedagogic work of teachers. Students do not come to school to learn what they already know.

Fourthly, it is teachers, in their pedagogy, not curriculum designers, who draw on pupils' everyday knowledge in helping them to engage with the concepts stipulated by the curriculum and to see their relevance. Finally, the knowledge stipulated by the curriculum must be based on specialist knowledge developed by communities of researchers. This process can be described as *curriculum recontextualization*. However, these research communities are not involved in schools. It follows that the curriculum cannot lay down how access to this knowledge is achieved; a further process of 'recontextualization' will be specific to each school and the community in which it is located and relies on the professional knowledge of teachers. Why then must the curriculum be subject based? This is the topic of the second half of this paper.

Subjects, the curriculum and the purposes of schooling

In this section, I want to shift my focus from the curriculum to the school and from curriculum designers to subject teachers. I draw here on the ideas of the French sociologist Bernard Charlot. He starts with the school and what kind of place it is. I will extract five related steps in elaborating his argument.

Schools are places where the world is treated as an 'object of thought' and not as a 'place of experience'. Subjects such as history, geography and physics are the tools that teachers have for helping pupils make the step from experience to what the Russian psychologist, Vygotsky, referred to as 'higher forms of thought'. Subjects bring together 'objects of thought' as systematically related sets of 'concepts'.

Sometimes, these concepts have referents outside school, in the environment of the pupil's life, in a city like London, for example. However, pupils' relationships with the 'concept' of a city should be different to their relationship with their 'experience' of London as the city where they live.

It is important that the pupils do not confuse the London that the geography teacher talks about with the London in which they live. To a certain extent, it is the same city, but the pupil's relationship with it in the two cases is not the same. The London where they live is 'a place of experience'. London as an example of a city is 'an object of thought' or a 'concept'.

If pupils fail to grasp the difference between thinking about London as an example of the geographers' concept of a city and their experience of living in London, they will have problems learning geography, and by analogy, any school subject that seeks to take them beyond their experience. For example, the teacher might ask her class what the functions of the city of London are. This requires that the pupils think of the city in its role in government and business and not to just describe how they, their parents and their friends, experience living in the city.

This argument can be expressed in another way as follows. The 'theoretical' concepts of subjects like geography and the 'everyday' concepts that make up the experience that pupils bring to school are different and using them involves very different thought processes. Again, it was Vygotsky who first pointed out these differences. It is worth summarizing them.

Theoretical concepts have origins in specialist knowledge-producing communities, like physicists and geographers. These concepts have specific purposes in that they enable us to make reliable generalizations from particular cases and test our generalizations. Theoretical concepts are systematically related to each other (in subjects and disciplines) and are acquired consciously and voluntarily through pedagogy in schools, colleges and universities.

In contrast, everyday concepts are 'picked up' unconsciously by everyone in our daily lives and are acquired through experience in ad hoc ways for specific purposes related to particular problems in particular contexts.

They form the knowledge we need to live in society. Subjects, therefore, are sets of related theoretical concepts, such as the city and suburbs for urban geographers and geography teachers. They are also the forms of social organization that bring subject specialists together and give them their identities.

Sometimes, in geography as in other subjects, curriculum concepts do not have a referent in the environment of the pupil's life. Such concepts belong only to a specific world, constructed by specialist researchers involved in developing new knowledge. Good examples are atoms and electrons in science. On the other hand, because they have been tried and tested by specialists, access to them is the most reliable way we have of extending a student's understanding.

Charlot concludes that teachers have two fundamental pedagogic tasks. One task is to help students manage the relationship between the concepts of the different subjects that make up the curriculum and their referents to the students' everyday lives. The second task is to introduce students to concepts, which have meanings that do not derive from or relate directly to their experience.

Subjects, then, have two features as a basis of curriculum design. First, they consist of relatively coherent sets of concepts with distinct and explicit relationships with each other. Different subjects have rules that define boundaries between them and other subjects and for how their concepts are related. These rules will vary in how precisely they are defined. The English sociologist of education, Basil Bernstein uses the concepts 'hierarchical' and 'segmented' to distinguish between subjects like physics and literature. Secondly, subjects are also 'communities of specialists' with distinct histories and traditions. Through these 'communities', teachers in different schools and colleges are linked to each other and to those in the universities producing new knowledge. Increasingly, they also link teachers in different countries through journals and conferences and the internet.

Two features distinguish this view of subjects, which is associated with what I referred to as a 'curriculum of engagement' from the traditionalist view of subjects associated with a 'curriculum of compliance'. The first is that subjects are dynamic historical entities that change over time, partly through internal development by specialists, and partly under external political and other pressures. In contrast to the traditional view of subjects, they are not part of some fixed canon defined by tradition with unchanging contents. This does not mean that it is possible to have a subject or a discipline without some form of the 'canon' of agreed texts, concepts and methods. It means that the canon itself has a history and, though not fixed and unchangeable, has a stability as well as an openness that students can build on in establishing their identities.

The second difference is that in acquiring subject knowledge students do not just comply with specific rules and contents as if they were instructions. In acquiring subject knowledge they are joining those 'communities of specialists' each with their different histories, traditions and ways of working. Subjects therefore have three roles in a 'curriculum of engagement'. The first is a curriculum role. Subjects provide guarantees, through their links with disciplines and the production of new knowledge, that students have access to the most reliable knowledge that is available in particular fields. The second role is a pedagogic one. Subjects provide bridges for learners to move from their 'everyday concepts' to the 'theoretical concepts' associated with different subjects.

The third is an identity-generating role for teachers and learners. Subjects are crucial for teachers' sense of themselves as members of a profession. Subject knowledge provides teachers with the basis of their authority over pupils. For pupils, moving from their everyday world where concepts are developed experientially in relation to problems that arise in specific contexts, to the world of school, which treats the world as an object for thinking about, can be a threatening and even alien experience. The everyday world is not like school. It is not divided into subjects or disciplines. This identity-generating role of subjects is particularly important for students from disadvantaged homes and for their teachers. Many such students will come to school with little experience of treating the world as more than a set of experiences, in other words, conceptually. Subjects, with their boundaries for separating aspects of the world that have been tested over time, not only provide the basis for analysing and asking questions about the world, they also provide students with the social basis for a new set of identities as learners. With the new subject identities that student's acquire through the curriculum, to add to those they came to school with, students are more likely to be able to resist, or at least cope with, the sense of alienation from their everyday lives outside school that school can lead to.

As a former chemistry teacher and lecturer in sociology, I have some idea of chemistry's concepts, like periodicity and valency, and those of sociology, like solidarity and social class. Such concepts, the relationships between them and to the world of everyday life have their own subject histories. They are what constitute subjects and provide the most powerful ways we have of generalizing beyond our experience of the world. It is for this reason that I argue for subjects as the basis of the curriculum.

Conclusions and challenges

I have developed an argument for the key role of subjects in the school curriculum and indicated some of the reasons why this role has been undermined by recent curriculum developments. A number of issues, however, remain.

In many countries, a non-subject-based curriculum based on themes, lines of enquiry or topics derived from the interests of pupils is being attempted and has proved attractive to teachers and pupils. It appears to resolve the issues of curriculum relevance and 'pupil interest' and the experience of subjects as a form of 'cultural tyranny'. My argument has been that such curricula, which quite explicitly blur the curriculum/pedagogy distinction, will inevitably lack coherence and be limited as a basis for pupils to progress. The basis for choosing topics or themes would be largely arbitrary or based on the experience of individual teachers not on the specialist subject knowledge of teachers and researchers developed over time.

In such a curriculum, teachers would have to rely more on their positional authority in the school and not on their specialist subject knowledge. Furthermore, the students could have difficulties in establishing their identities as school learners and would incline either to personal loyalty to specific teachers or reject the teacher's positional authority as bureaucratic and illegitimate, the beginnings of disaffection that often leads to drop out. Despite these problems, support for an integrated or thematic curriculum is unlikely to disappear, especially among 'radical' teachers. Such curricula appear to offer a way of overcoming the overspecialization problem; how, in a subject-based curriculum do students acquire the resources to 'make connections' and gain a sense of the world as a 'whole'? This issue is important but beyond the scope of this chapter. I will, therefore, restrict myself to some brief observations. The 'connection' problem has no easy solution, and there is no evidence that intellectual specialization is likely to go into reverse. For schools, I suggest, it is a pedagogic not a curriculum problem. In curriculum terms, there is no adequate alternative to subjects for stipulating the concepts that we want students to acquire. There are no general 'connecting' curriculum principles that might give the idea of 'connective specialization' specific meaning. My provisional response is that the capability to connect or 'cross boundaries' can be encouraged by teachers and arises out of the strength of a student's subject identity and the problems that she or he finds that the subject-based concepts cannot adequately deal with.

There is a parallel point that needs exploring further that in the production of new knowledge 'a form of interdisciplinarity' is normal. It is an interdisciplinarity that arises out of the openness and its limitations of disciplines and not from some imposed external demand. In the context of the school, it is the subject teacher's responsibility to monitor, criticize and at times support those students who struggle to move beyond the boundaries between particular subjects.

I want finally to consider two rather different objections to my argument for a knowledge-based curriculum. The first is that, despite distinguishing between 'compliance' and 'engagement' curriculum models, my engagement model of a subject-based curriculum is very little different from the traditionalist curriculum supported by our new Secretary of State. In other words, it would inevitably perpetuate an elitist and unequal system and continue to deny learning opportunities to many students from disadvantaged homes. It is a familiar argument and is consistent with the critique of subjects that I made in my first book *Knowledge and Control*. However, as I discuss in Chapter 1, I was led to rethink my earlier ideas about knowledge, the curriculum and the role of schooling. This does not mean that I now disregard how schools in capitalist societies reproduce social class and other inequalities. However, the reality that *some* boys from working-class families do succeed at school despite their cultural disadvantages and that in many countries *girls do better than boys* despite gender discrimination in the society, suggests that the role of a subject-based curriculum is more complex than sustaining social class inequalities.

In unequal societies such as England, any school curriculum will sustain those inequalities. However, schooling also represents (or can represent, depending on the curriculum) the universalist goals of treating all pupils equally and not just as members of different social classes, different ethnic groups or as boys or girls.

Common schooling with the goal of maximizing the intellectual development of all students can be thought of as an institution like science, democracy and trade unions. None have fully realized the aims associated with them, but none are the products of capitalism, or colonialism and their divisions alone. Common schooling arose, in part, out of the needs of an expanding industrial capitalism and the social class inequalities that it generated. However, it was also a product of the eighteenth-century Enlightenment and the values of universalism and equality associated with it. Schools and the curriculum, like political institutions such as democracy and trade unions are in constant tension with their context. They are not just products of that context.

It would be naïve to imagine that any curriculum could overcome inequalities generated elsewhere. Capitalist societies, to different degrees will always produce inequalities in education, health, housing or any public service. On the other hand, a subject-based curriculum has a degree of objectivity based on the assumption that it is the most reliable way we have developed of transmitting and acquiring 'powerful knowledge'. No one would imagine that the creation of new knowledge could begin with experience or everyday life. Isaac Newton is reported to have said, *'If I have seen further it is only by standing on the shoulders of giants.'* It is no less true of acquiring knowledge. Subjects link the acquisition of new knowledge to its production. To deny this in the curriculum is no different from denying access to anti-retrovirals to Africans with HIV Aids on the grounds that it shows lack of respect for their local knowledge.

We can link this argument back to my earlier account of subjects. On average, middle-class families give their children more experiences of treating the world 'as an object' or in a way that has some parallels with subjects and not just as an experience, than working-class families; not surprisingly the former are better prepared for a subject-based curriculum. We can call this a middle-class subsidy. At the same time, subjects with their sequencing, pacing, and selection of contents and activities, are the nearest we get in education to providing students with access to reliable knowledge. In other words, at their best school subjects express universal values that treat all human beings as the same, not as members of different social classes, ethnic groups, or as boys or girls. Elite schools are successful for two reasons. The first is the ability that charging high fees gives them to be both socially and intellectually selective. The second is that they have the resources to recruit the best teachers of specialist subject teachers. The lack of well-qualified subject teachers is a major reason why, in relative terms, state schools do not do so well. Weakening the subject basis of the curriculum will make it more difficult for students to distinguish between the 'objects of thought' or concepts that constitute a curriculum and their experience. One reason why our current Secretary of State is wrong is that he endorses a universalistic goal, 'subject teachers should treat all learners equally', in a non-universalistic context: not all students have the same access to specialist subject teachers.

A second objection to my reconceptualized subject-based 'curriculum for engagement' is that it takes no account of the global transformations of society that have and are taking place. Here, I can only hint at my response; it needs another paper. Weakening boundaries between school subjects and everyday knowledge is often presented as consistent with political and economic transformations associated with globalization. Parallels can be drawn with the recent enthusiasm for the idea that the production of new knowledge is shifting from disciplinary to transdisciplinary forms. The case is then made for a transdisciplinary or thematic school curriculum as being more in tune with the world 'as it is becoming'.

Producing new knowledge by research and acquiring it through formal education are relatively recent phenomena in human history. There is a relevant body of research which can be traced back to the work of the French sociologist, Emile Durkheim. He argued that differentiating between knowledge and experience and between theoretical and everyday knowledge are the most basic conditions for acquiring and producing new knowledge (Durkheim, 1983; Young, 2008).

I will conclude with an observation from Max Weber, the German sociologist. He wrote that:

> In Western civilisation, and in Western civilisation only, cultural phenomena have appeared (and the subject-based curriculum could be thought of as one, though he did not refer to it) which . . . lie in a line of development having universal significance and validity.

For some readers, trying to extract a set of ideas from their political and historical context and claiming their universality might sound like a form of neo-colonialism. However, I think Weber was raising another question with very deep implications for those who work in education. The question goes something like this: What are the educational implications of there being some knowledge which has generalizable meanings and a degree of objectivity that cannot be reduced to its contexts or origins? In other words, Weber is writing about the idea of truth, or as I express it in an earlier chapter of this book, truth as the best knowledge we have in any field of enquiry. If subjects are the nearest we get in a curriculum to having access to this 'best knowledge', are there any grounds for denying access to such knowledge to the next generation, whatever their social or cultural backgrounds or the pace of their learning.

5

Curriculum change and control: A headteacher's perspective

Martin Roberts

In this chapter which draws on reflections following 30 years in schools, including service as a comprehensive school headteacher and then as a member of the steering committee of the Prince's Teaching Institute, I aim to show how liberal education principles, subject knowledge and teacher professionalism have been undermined. I go on to say why I am convinced that the idea of 'powerful knowledge', and the right of access to this to all students as proposed in Future 3 schools, is important in the never ending process of educational change.

In this chapter therefore, there is an inevitable element of looking back: this chapter is meant to provide a personal historical perspective on where we have come from. The framework of alternative 'Futures' we have used in this book is very useful in preventing a misreading of this. Although we analyse some things that have been lost we are not harking back, perhaps with rose tinted spectacles, to a Future 1. My account, which I hope shows the pragmatic concern of headteachers to make things work for the benefit of students and staff as well as more idealistic underpinnings of educational principles, possibly betrays a growing frustration. In a nutshell, the limitations of what we now call Future 1 were evident, not least as so many young people appeared to be let down by their school experience. But the solutions, collectively referred to as Future 2, became deeply unconvincing to me as a headteacher. The prospect of grasping a knowledge-led alternative in the shape of Future 3 is clearly challenging, but well worth trying. It requires headteachers and their staff teams to reopen the question: what are schools for? As the school system in England (and elsewhere) is academicized and local responsibilities for the curriculum are increased it is a good time to ask the question.

Setting the scene: An initial broad sweep

In the last decades of the twentieth century, what can genuinely be described as a revolution took place in English education. Governments, Labour following Conservative in 1997, took control of the curriculum from teachers, mortally wounded local education authorities by shifting most of their powers either to central government or to schools and instituted a powerful system of accountability for individual schools in the form of the central inspection agency Ofsted. They also decided to measure school effectiveness and to try to secure a nationwide improvement of standards by setting targets primarily in terms of results achieved in national tests at 11, 14, 16 and 18. These changes also significantly affected the work of the examination system and the links between universities and schools. As far as the curriculum is concerned, one effect of this revolution was to end, temporarily we hope, debates among teachers about curriculum principles. Governments decided what the curriculum should be. The task of teachers was to implement it.

Alex Moore (2006) has recalled how in the 1970s he and his colleagues in the English department of a large inner-city comprehensive took it for granted that they should keep abreast of the wide range of publications on curricular issues, and would discuss their practical implications at professional development sessions laid on either by their own school or by their local education authority specialist adviser. How things have changed he noted, when 'in one of our major retailers of educational books . . . its shelves are currently filled with guides, practice booklets and "cribs" at the expense of books which seek to examine and discuss different models and intentions of curriculum design' (Moore, 2006: 2). However, while major retailers of educational books in 2013 still stock plenty of 'practice booklets, cribs and guides to school improvement', it is not difficult to find publications which address more deeply various curriculum issues which take us very directly to fundamental questions about the role of schools and what it means to be educated in this day and age. As well as Michael Young's *Bringing Knowledge Back In* (2008), there are many others such as Richard Pring's *The Life and Death of Secondary Education for All* (2013). Various reports are also easily available such as *The Nuffield Review Education for All* (2009), Tim Oates' *Could Do Better* (2010) and Alison Wolf's *Review of Vocational Education* (2011).

These are lively but also enduring discussions about the same central issue that has been a part of my entire professional career – whether there can be a common curriculum for all pupils and if so what should be its characteristics. History does not repeat itself but it can provide perspectives on the present from which those planning the future can usefully learn. My time as a headteacher coincided with the educational revolution described earlier, which was an element in a much wider upheaval in the relationship between government, the public sector and the professionals who ran that sector. We are now living with the consequences of that upheaval and when the neo-liberal ideology that drove it is being strongly contested. As a new generation of teachers seeks better ways of educating a new generation of pupils, these perspectives from the past may be helpful.

Becoming a headteacher and curriculum responsibilities

My first teaching post was at Leeds Grammar School, now an independent school. Like many young grammar school teachers of that time, I was inspired by the comprehensive ideal. It seemed to us that comprehensivization should substantially increase the life opportunities of the less well-off, improve social mobility and weaken the class structure which blights British society. I moved first to a comprehensive school in Harlow as head of history and then in 1974 to Sandy in Bedfordshire as deputy head of a brand new 13–18 community upper school. I became head of the Cherwell School in Oxford in 1981.

The ideal of a 'liberal' education underpinned the curriculum of school I attended as a pupil, the undergraduate teaching of my university and the grammar school in which a started my career. That liberal education was in most respects a version of Future 1 but it had an important vision of what should be the main purpose of education. Richard Pring describes it well drawing on the metaphor of a 'conversation' used by the philosopher Michael Oakeshott. Education is a conversation between the learner, aided by the teacher, and what others have said and done. 'Liberal learning is an initiation into the art of this conversation in which we learn to recognise the voices of science, of history, of poetry, of religion, of philosophy and to distinguish their mode of utterance' (Pring, 2013: 33). As a consequence of this initiation, young people gain an understanding of the world in which they are growing up and an awareness of the potential of their society both to do good and to do harm. The knowledge and the critical powers that it imparts enable them to function as free citizens in a representative democracy. That is a key characteristic of a 'liberal' education, part of what Pring describes as 'moral seriousness'.

Sally Tomlinson (2001) explains clearly the curricular challenges which newly created comprehensive schools faced. The grammar school offer had been 'a traditional academic education, secondary modern schools attempted to develop post-elementary prevocational education. Comprehensive schools became a mixture of the two traditions, although many comprehensive schools did attempt to implement a common curriculum, and teachers began to search for ways in which courses for pupils previously written off academically' (Tomlinson, 2001: 37). The creation of a comprehensive school curriculum was our aim when we opened Sandy Upper School in 1974. We believed in the merits of a liberal subject-based education for all – that it would provide pupils with the necessary disciplined and critical understanding of the world they would soon enter. We were influenced by the ideas in Phenix's 'realms of meaning' (Phenix, 1964) and Hirst's 'areas of experience' (Hirst, 1974) and aimed to provide a broad and balanced curriculum. We decided against hybrid subjects like 'integrated humanities' which were then popular since we believed that unless they were particularly well designed they would lack rigour.

The Cherwell School in Oxford was completing the transition from 'secondary modern' to comprehensive when I became headteacher. My aim was to create a common, broad and balanced subject-based curriculum not dissimilar to the one which we had developed in Bedfordshire. By today's standards it is staggering the degree of control I could exert with my colleagues over the curriculum: 'our' curriculum was unequivocally ours. It appeared inconceivable that central government might wish to take that control from us. We had all grown up with a general assumption, shared by politicians and the general public, that the curriculum was the concern of individual schools and government interference was in principle wrong.

LEAs were then powerful and often led curriculum initiatives as well as leading CPD through their specialist subject advisers and teachers' centres. At a national level the Schools Council provided non-directive leadership for the development of the curriculum and examinations. Subject associations like the

Association for Science Education (ASE) and the Historical Association (HA), also provided CPD. Teachers were also much involved and influential in the 'examination boards' most of which still had close links with their founding universities. As Pring puts it, this was 'a period when teachers were in the driving seat, where development depended on their research and co-operation' (Pring, 2013: 119).

The arrival of the National Curriculum in 1988

Within Westminster however the mood towards state-funded education and school autonomy was changing. The changing mood affected much more than just education. By and large the 1970s were a bad time for the United Kingdom and its citizens' morale. It was a decade of acute economic crises, of the oil price hike, of frequent and damaging strikes, especially in the nationalized industries, of three day weeks and the 'winter of discontent' of 1978–9 when a series of strikes by public sector workers caused widespread disruption with rubbish lying uncollected for weeks in city streets. The Conservative Party, notably its rising stars Margaret Thatcher and Sir Keith Joseph, were much influenced by the neo-liberal ideas of Friedrich von Hayek who argued that prosperity, progress and liberty depended on the market operating as freely as possible and that the more competition could be introduced to major public enterprises like health and education the better. A related neo-liberal assumption was, as David Marquand puts it in his eloquent defence of the public sector ethos *The Decline of the Public*, 'that professions were at bottom self-interested producer cartels, seeking monopoly rents' (Marquand, 2004).

The Conservatives under Mrs Thatcher took office in 1979 and Sir Keith Joseph became Secretary of State for Education. He abolished the Schools Council in 1982 replacing it with two government appointed committees, the SEC (the School Examination Council) and the SCDC (the School Curriculum Development Council) to oversee the curriculum and examinations. The numerous GCE and CSE examination boards in England were subsumed into first four and later three much larger examining groups. In these new examining groups the direct influence of universities was diluted.

Detailed top-down control of the curriculum by central government dates from the Education Reform Acts of 1988 to 1991 which the Conservative government passed after its victory in the 1987 general election. That central control was sustained and intensified by subsequent governments. Kenneth Baker justified the introduction of a government-controlled national curriculum in 1987. It was needed he said to ensure a broad and balanced curriculum which had coherence and was expressive of national standards.

Between Baker and his prime minister there was considerable tension. Though an enthusiast for technological education, Baker loved history and poetry. He understood that a 'liberal' education mattered. Thatcher, a trained chemist, had a more pragmatic instrumental approach. Better education through the National Curriculum must contribute to economic growth. The former believed strongly in the need for breadth and balance including history, geography and the creative subjects. Mrs Thatcher preferred a simpler core curriculum of English, maths and science. Initially, at one point threatening to resign, Baker got his way. However, the whole process then spun out of control with a plethora of Programmes of Study, Attainment Targets, Levels of Attainment and Standard Assessment Tasks (SATs). Schools came to dread the arrival of the latest ring-binders from the Department of Education and Science. Secretaries of State came and went in quick succession and the NUT boycotted the Key Stage 3 SATs. What ministers and the DfE failed to notice, curiously, was if that pupils took all the core and foundation subjects to GCSE as the subject working parties defining the details of the new curriculum assumed, they simply could not be crammed into a school's working week; a striking example of trying to get a quart into a pint pot.

So in 1993, John Patten, then Secretary of State, appointed Sir Ron Dearing, a former chairman of the Post Office, to sort out the mess. Dearing's version was much closer to the Thatcher preference than Baker's broad and balanced vision. Once the government had defined a compulsory core and increasingly judged schools on their examination results, headteachers inevitably looked to strengthening their 'core' subjects and marginalizing the others. Ofsted replaced HMI in 1993 and its systematic and judgemental programme of school inspections, monitoring school curricula and increasingly and publicly emphasizing the importance of exam results as the measure of school improvement forced schools to take careful note of government priorities.

Once central government takes control of the curriculum, whom it appoints to decide what should be taught is a matter of some significance. Kenneth Baker aimed to appoint working parties consisting of leading subject specialists but some of these groups found it hard to find a consensus. In English the battlegrounds were the teaching of grammar and the 'canon' of English literature; in music the balance between classical, folk and rock music. Much the most controversial subject however was history in which the media was greatly interested, in particular how much and what British history should be taught and did skills like interpretation and empathy matter more than the acquisition of facts. Mrs Thatcher wanted a more patriotic version than the one which eventually emerged in 1991 and history teachers were up in arms over the dangers of the national history curriculum becoming politically biased.

New Labour 1997 Instrumentalism (Future 2) gathers pace

To the surprise of many teachers who voted for them in 1997, most of Labour education policies continued those of the Conservatives only more intensively. When Tony Blair campaigned on 'education, education, education' the kind of education he had in mind was unambiguously 'technical–instrumental'.

As David Blunkett, Blair's first Secretary of State for Education put it, 'we are talking about investing in human capital in an age of knowledge. To compete in the global economy . . . we have to unlock the potential of every young person.' For Michael Barber who headed the Standards and Effectiveness Unit at the DfEE Labour was on a crusade to make the English education system 'world class'. What was needed was a step-change in policies and attitudes. The measure of world class was how England stood in such international league tables as enumerated in such international measures like PISA and TIMMS (Trends in International Mathematics and Science Study). Targets, tests and 'league' tables of results which the newspapers loved were the levers for achieving the step-change. Ofsted inspections became more frequent, particularly of struggling schools. Test results became the dominant measure of school improvement. As for the National Curriculum, the revised version of 2000 reflected the government instrumental philosophy since its introduction read:

> The function of education above all is to ensure that all pupils respond as individuals, parents, workers and citizens to the rapid expansion of communication technologies, changing roles of employment and new work and leisure patterns resulting from economic migration and the continual globalisation of the economy and society. (DfEE, 1999)

In this 2000 revision, greater emphasis was laid on literacy, numeracy and key skills including ICT. A particular interest of David Blunkett was citizenship and he persuaded his old university tutor Bernard Crick to devise a programme for schools. Initially Crick intended teachers of subjects like history, geography, business studies and English to teach citizenship issues across the curriculum but eventually Blunkett ruled that it must be given 5 per cent of curriculum time and GCSEs in citizenship and at A level soon appeared. While many schools took up citizenship enthusiastically and the GCSE courses quickly had many takers, schools varied greatly in their attitude to the subject and in how they timetabled it. Its compulsory introduction added another element to an already crowded curriculum and put a further squeeze on the humanities and the creative subjects.

A substantial innovation for sixth-formers was Curriculum 2000, the introduction of AS levels into sixth forms. Its intention was to broaden the Y12 curriculum, pupils being encouraged to take four AS and reduce to three A2s in Y13. AS had a modular structure in contrast to the linear two-year A levels which it replaced, reinforcing a culture of 'teaching to the test' in schools right up to including A levels, with students and their teachers focused on the module examinations and the accumulation of points, repeating modules if necessary.

Changes to vocational and prevocational courses

In 1980 the main providers of vocational courses were City and Guilds and the RSA. BTEC joined them in 1984. Since then government spokespersons from every party have insisted on the importance of more pupils taking better vocational qualifications and for them to 'gain parity of esteem' with academic ones.

That has not happened. In a chapter titled 'A Great Idea for Other People's Children: The Decline and Fall of Vocational Education' in her *Does Education Matter?* (2003), Alison Wolf describes how despite great endeavour and much expenditure, a succession of government initiatives foundered. Government's activist policies in the 1980s and 1990s, she writes, 'were in a large part about extending central-government power. Vocational qualifications had been effectively unnationalized and unregulated. . . . The reformers at the Department of Employment, the MSC and the National Council for Vocational Qualifications (NCVQ) believed that they could do better and increase demand, quality and economic relevance by developing tight, clear, national frameworks. They also thought that they could definitively alter teenagers', parents' and employers' views of the relative value and desirability of the different sorts of education. (Wolf, 2003: 93)

Wolf explains that the new qualifications, whether they were NVQs or GNVQs or Applied GCSEs or post-2005 Diplomas, were for the most part too complicated and bureaucratic. They did not recognize the demographic trend that more pupils were going to stay on at school and aim for university and that changes in the global and national economy made academic qualifications for the majority a more attractive route into the job market than specifically vocational ones. In order to make GNVQs more attractive, the Department for Education gave them spurious equivalencies with established GCSE courses. Not surprisingly many schools adopted them as much for their contribution to 'better' GCSE results and a higher position in the annual school league tables. Under New Labour the number of pupils taking vocational qualification like BTEC and Applied GCSEs rose from 15,000 to 575,000 and the proportion of GCSEs achieved through Applied GCSEs and 'equivalent' vocational courses rose proportionately. In 2005 only 5.1 per cent of the A*–C passes were in vocational qualifications by 2010 that proportion had risen to 19.1 per cent (Wolf, 2003: 49).

Warwick Mansell, in his *Education by Numbers: The Tyranny of Testing* (2007), describes the success of Thomas Telford School in Shropshire in designing an IT GNVQ course which had the equivalent of four GCSEs which it then sold very profitably to other schools. Mansell also analysed the results of some of the schools singled out by the Department of Education in 2004 as the most 'improved' secondaries (Mansell, 2007: 118). In the majority, the improvement was clearly the consequence of entering a much higher proportion of pupils for GNVQs rather than conventional GCSEs. That may well have been in the educational interest of some but not others for whom conventional GCSEs would have been a much better for progression into the Sixth Form.

It was not surprising therefore that when Alison Wolf reported to the new Coalition government (Wolf, 2011) it speedily reduced the number of such approved courses from over 3,000 to 70. We are no nearer to creating vocational qualifications popular with pupils and 'with parity of esteem' than we were in 1980. In the meantime there has been a comparative decline in the numbers taking more 'academic' GSCEs like history, geography and MFL. For example, by 2010 more than 100 schools entered no pupils for GCSE History which was seen as a difficult GCSE while geography and MFL have seen a drop in their GCSE numbers in recent years.

The impact of policy change on the Cherwell School

I was not really aware of the implications of the changing national mood about education in the early 1980s. My concerns as a new head were local. School rolls were falling in Oxford as fast as elsewhere and there were too many secondary schools. Cherwell's reputation was not specially high. We were losing many pupils from our neighbourhood to other state schools, especially to the ex-grammar schools and to the strong independent sector in Oxford. My priority was stabilizing our numbers (630 for a 13–18 upper school) and if possible to increase them. At the same time as introducing a broad and balanced curriculum, we had to concentrate on improving our exam results, especially at A and O level. I was pleased to be part of the (in full with date) LAPP initiative, short-lived though it was, since the additional funding enabled us to involve our most disadvantaged pupils in practical and outdoor activities, a high point being their visits to Oxfordshire's activities centre on the Gower peninsula. We were also able to purchase a Leyland bus for a hands-on motor mechanics course.

Like most of my colleagues I was initially shocked when I realized that the government was serious about instituting a National Curriculum. Such a policy attacked directly the culture of teacher control which my generation had taken for granted. In conjunction with the other elements of the Education Reform Acts of 1988–92, especially local management of schools, it transformed the responsibilities of headteachers. My interest was primarily the curriculum and the governors had appointed me to improve the school's curriculum and examination results, especially at A level. I now found myself with only limited scope for curriculum development but daunting and unexpected new responsibilities for the budget, buildings and personnel.

On reflection though I decided that having a National Curriculum was a sensible idea, assuming that the government's active role would be limited, the provision perhaps of a national framework, but supervised by a mainly expert educationist body, at arms length from the government. Of that naïve assumption I was soon disabused. I did not fully comprehend how deep was the Thatcher's government's distrust of 'the educational establishment'.

Our whole school broad and balanced subject-based curriculum seemed theoretically compatible with the first Kenneth Baker model but the Dearing slimmed-down version which took effect from 1993 posed us real problems. In order to sustain humanities and creative options we decided not to require all pupils to take MFL nor CDT. Our thinking was also influenced by more pragmatic in-house factors. With MFL we had approximately 75 per cent take-up and were not convinced of the value of making it compulsory for the remaining 25 per cent, most of whom had problems with their own language. With CDT, take-up post-14 was low because our secondary modern trained department of woodwork, metalwork and technical drawing struggled to adjust to CDT and I had found it almost impossible to find good additional staff. On balance, I preferred pupils being able to choose subjects in which they would thrive with excellent teaching rather than forcing them to take a subject of undoubted curricular value but of which their experience of which would almost certainly be negative.

Since by 1993 we were heavily oversubscribed and our governors did not mind our being in breach of the regulations, I thought we would persuade Ofsted of appropriateness of our non-compliant curriculum. In this we failed. Our first inspectors rapped our knuckles and told us that we must obey the regulations. Since we ignored that instruction, we wondered what would be the outcome of the second inspection which followed five years later. Fortunately I was able to argue, accurately as it turned out, that the word from QCA (which by then had replaced SCAA) was that soon MFL and CDT would become optional so surely compliance to the soon to be superseded regulations would be pointless.

As for vocational and prevocational education, our experience with TVEI made me uneasy about the manner in which the government was developing and emphasizing the importance of their initiatives. I attended frequent meetings with a succession of business leaders in school–business partnerships but sustained collaboration proved elusive. Among our pupils vocational courses had limited demand. We offered to our one year sixth City and Guilds 365 but could not get it off the ground for lack of numbers. With Certificate of Pre-Vocational Education we were more successful only for that to be withdrawn as a national qualification in 1990. Since the Oxford College of Further Education (OCFE) was only a mile away, we were able to send a small number of pupils to participate in 14–16 courses there and would advise pupils who were sure that they wished to pursue a vocational option to transfer to the OCFE at 16 as we could not realistically compete with their course offers and facilities.

The introduction of the top-down National Curriculum had two obviously damaging effects. My English department was outstanding and as a team had created its own 100 per cent coursework GCSE. Before long, national regulation outlawed such courses and my brilliant creative head of department left the profession in disgust. The other damage was less obvious but cumulative. Instead carefully evolving our policies with our governors who understood local needs, we found ourselves essentially stationary, having to react to frequently changing national initiatives, many of them ill-considered. I remember feeling increasing frustration as yet another policy document arrived from the DfE and having to judge whether or not it could go straight into the waste paper basket. With school budgets kept under tight control, we looked for government initiatives which would release funds to us without compromising our curriculum. An example of this was 'specialist' status. Neither my governors nor I saw the desirability of specialisms but we decided that if we succeeded in achieving science specialist status that would generate additional funds with virtually no impact on our curriculum structure, so that is what we did.

It was in applying for specialist status that I became aware of the 'equivalences' game headteachers were beginning to play. While I was completing the bid for specialist status I had a phone conversation with a consultant. I thought the target for improved GCSE results was rather demanding and asked for his advice. 'No problem', he said, 'change to some Applied GCSEs and your results will rise much higher than that target'. When I demurred saying I did not see that such a change was clearly in the pupils' interest, his reply was to the effect the 'then you do have a problem'. Like many headteachers I visited Thomas Telford School and was much impressed by their description of their IT course. However, when I suggested to my head of IT that we might introduce it he checked it out and came back adamantly against. In his view it seriously lacked rigour. Our response to citizenship was similar. We thought its examination syllabuses light-weight and surprisingly weak on political literacy.

Reflections after 20 years as a headteacher

Curriculum change

Despite the many national changes described earlier, the Cherwell curriculum hardly changed over 20 years because pupils, parents and governors liked it and the school was seen as successful. The school grew as an upper school from 633 in 1981 of whom 120 were sixth-formers to 1,020 in 2002 of whom 300 were sixth-formers. Now it is an 11–18 school of 1,800 with a sixth form of nearly 500. In the 20 years of Ofsted, the school has been rated either good with outstanding features or outstanding even if we ignored some of the National Curriculum requirement. The exam results improved steadily rather than spectacularly. In the county league tables the school was usually around sixth or seventh for GCSE, first or second for A level.

However while in 1981 we decided what was best for our pupils, from 1988 we were having to defend what we had created for the reasons stated rather than plan together how we might improve what we had achieved. We continued to believe in a broad and balanced subject-based curriculum. After 1993 central government did not and from 1997 pursued a powerful instrumentalist agenda, which Ofsted monitored more and more powerfully.

The situation of headteachers of less fortunate schools was quite different. Getting up the league tables by better test results became the priority; hence the popularity of BTEC and GNVQ and the decline in the take-up of academic GCSEs. Survival depended on maintaining or increasing pupil numbers, which meant in turn rising in the league tables and getting a good Ofsted report. From 2002, Ofsted judgements were firmly based on quantitative test data. In such circumstances a liberal broad-based curriculum was seen by many headteachers as out of date because that is how the government regarded it.

The undermining of subject knowledge

Since both GCSE and A level remained subject-based, the undermining of subject knowledge was hard to detect apart from the flight to GVVQs/Applied GCSEs in many schools. At Cherwell, virtually all teachers taught A level as well as Key Stages 3 and 4. The school's reputation depended more on its A level results and numbers entering Russell group universities than any other single factor, so our teachers had to be high quality and committed subject specialists.

However, we noticed as time passed what perhaps can best be described as the narrowing or desiccation of knowledge and the discouragement of inspired and creative subject teaching because of the changes in the way examining groups set their exams and advised teachers how to prepare for them. Mansell (2007) is essential reading here. He explains how the competing examining groups have described in ever greater detail their exam specifications and how, because of the pressures on them from the national 'hyper-accountability regime' of the inescapable league tables and of Ofsted, teachers teach to the test in increasing numbers. He describes the use of writing frames, of 'booster' materials, of months of revision and exam repeats, the obsession with pupils on the C/D borderline, malpractice with regard to coursework, expensive courses run by examiners providing tips to maximize their pupils' grades and the textbook market becoming dominated by books written by examiners which are essentially guides about how to perform well in relation to the specifications, not to a deep and rounded understanding of the subject.

In 2005 the Mathematical Association commented: 'The current assessment system, backed by the accountability structure, encourages a mode of preparation for tests and examinations which focuses solely on the standard questions that appears on the papers. . . . This leads to the exclusion of more interesting and challenging problems and applications at all levels. These are the very things that are of importance to employers and higher education, because they stimulate interest and encourage independent thinking' (Mansell, 2007: 61).

A sixth-former studying history in 2009 expressed a similar view to the authors of the *Nuffield Review of 14–19 Education and Training*:

Far too often the emphasis is on achieving targets and regurgitating what the exam board wants, as to actually teaching children something. As a sixth form student myself, this frustrates me on a daily basis, especially in history, when we must write to the specifications of the exam board, rather than actually learning about the past.

Mansell's evidence that teachers felt depressingly constrained and powerless to change the 'teaching to the test' culture is overwhelming.

The undermining of teacher professionalism

It is hard to imagine just how free teachers were in the 1980s in curricular matters. In 2003, Julian Le Grand published his *Motivation, Agency and Public Policy* about politicians and the public sector. The key question for politicians was 'should public workers be thought of more as "knights" motivated mainly by the desire to do their best for their clients or "knaves" guided mainly by self-interest' (Le Grand, 2003). Le Grand, who advised Tony Blair on public sector reform, believed that before Mrs Thatcher the public regarded teachers as knights but she thought them more as knaves. Le Grand, perhaps reflecting Blair's position, was not sure whether or not they were predominantly knavish but he was sure that a powerful accountability system was essential to limit any knavish tendencies. So New Labour increased the powers of Ofsted and not only determined what teachers should teach but also how. The most striking examples of this were at primary level with the national literacy and numeracy standards but at secondary as well as primary teachers became convinced that there was an Ofsted-approved way. Make sure that you have a three- or four-stage lesson with the objectives listed on the whiteboard. Never talk for more than 10 minutes in a lesson. Consultants told senior leaders what Ofsted was looking for and these leaders observed lessons to check that they were what their consultants told them were Ofsted-compliant.

The most obvious criticism of central control by contemporary politicians is that they are usually short-termist with the next election pending and, driven by spin and 24/7 news, too prone to shiny bright new initiatives which will give a superficial impression of drive and authority. While I was a headteacher the initiatives, some of them mentioned in this chapter came and went with a life span of just a few years. Building and sustaining a world-class education service with such major discontinuities is impossible. We should restore a consensus that teachers are more usually knights rather than knaves who can and should through their professional expertise determine those curricular policies which will prove durable in serving both national needs and who can adapt themselves over time to changing circumstances.

The Princes Teaching Institute, Michael Young and identifying Future 3

On retiring from my headship in 2002, I joined the steering group which created the Prince's Teaching Institute (PTI). The origins of the PTI lay in the concern Prince Charles had for the teaching of English literature and history. He feared that 'there is a danger that we are creating a society in which children, wherever they come from, will have a diminishing chance to understand their place in history, the significance of culture and ideas which they have inherited, the nature of their own identity, and the distinction between the good and bad, the creative and the mediocre'. He therefore established a residential Summer School for state school teachers of English literature and history.

At first sight the PTI looks elitist and Future 1, and it has had its critics for this reason. However, elitist it is not. Our aim is to give encouragement to all those teachers who believe that subject expertise is essential to inspirational teaching and that they must keep in touch with the university scholars in their discipline who are driving their subject forward. PTI courses are 'designed by teachers for teachers' and involve numerous colleagues from universities.

Initially the PTI concentrated on residential Summer Schools for teachers of English and History. We invited scholars like Simon Schama and Seamus Heaney, organized workshops led by outstanding teacher practitioners, shared good practice and at the end of each conference enabled the participants to meet with important education policy makers including politicians from both parties so that they could put to them issues arising from the course which they wanted to share with them.

The PTI's teacher leaders concentrated on what they thought made good teaching. The courses avoided mention of current bugbears like testing and Ofsted. Teachers who took part almost without exception valued the offer and through discussion improved it. The PTI's offer thus expanded to include Science, Maths, Geography, MFL and most recently Art and Music. Out of the Summer Schools came the Schools Programme in which, during the year following the Summer Schools' teachers would undertake a project which would enhance subject learning in their school. From 2006 formal links with the University of Cambridge were established as the PTI extended its operations. Thus, daylong subject-centred CPD was started with a similar balance of activities to the Summer Schools, and from 2010 conferences for headteachers with the focus on how to encourage high-quality subject teaching. In 2011, courses for NQTs were introduced requiring the commitment of six Saturdays during the school year. By working with experienced teacher leaders and sharing good practice with their peers drawn from across the country, they increased their expertise and confidence.

The PTI grows and participants in courses continue to appreciate what is being provided. By 2013 its alumni were coming from more than a quarter of the schools in the country. More than 300 young teachers were giving up 6 Saturdays in a year to come to our Subject Days. The appetite for subject-based CPD is real and growing, as is the keenness to discuss together without a government or an Ofsted agenda what really they should be doing as professionals.

The initial criticism of PTI as elitist and conservative caused me to improve my knowledge of current curriculum theory. Colleagues pointed me towards writers like John White (2004) and Stephen Heppell (2006) who argued that the established 'academic' subjects were obsolete. Furthermore, because the internet, effortlessly accessed, held more knowledge than any one teacher could master, new curricula based on aims and values derived from the experience of young people should replace the subject-based curriculum of the nineteenth and twentieth century, and teachers instead of acting as instructors should guide pupils to the knowledge and understanding they needed through e-technology; the 'guide on the side' rather than 'the sage on the stage'. At the same time, the RSA Opening Minds initiative argued with much publicity that the future lay with a competences-based curriculum.

I could not accept these arguments. Widespread knowledge and understanding seem to me critically important defences against ignorance and tyranny. Such knowledge derives from subject specialists whose endeavours contribute to the survival of civilization and to social progress. In a genuine democracy such knowledge cannot be the privilege of an elite and the key responsibility of teachers is to enable all youngsters to share it at the highest level that they can manage. Many pupils will find some subjects difficult but as their knowledge and understanding progresses so their lives will be enhanced. This was the driving principle of the Cherwell curriculum and is also of the PTI's.

In recent years I looked for a modern equivalent of the books such as those by Phenix and Hirst which had inspired me as a young teacher and which would provide a contemporary rationale for a knowledge-led curriculum. Michael Young's *Bringing Knowledge Back In* offered to do this. Young's sociological analysis of recent curriculum development, from neo-conservative to technical–instrumental, reflects my own experience – and his 'social realist' Future 3 as described in Chapter 3 of this book suggests an alternative way forward for schools in the twenty-first century. As Young points out, instrumentalists criticize what they see as the obsolete subject-based curriculum for what they believe to be its elitism and resistance to change. But 'they fail to recognise that the social organisation of subjects and disciplines transcend its elitist origins as a basis of the acquisition of and production of knowledge' (Young, 2008: 33). The subject-based networks of university and school teachers, for example, through subject associations, are essential for 'objectivity and a sense of standards' which are in turn essential to high-quality education.

So, as increasingly autonomous schools build their new curricula, subject networks of university and school teachers need to work closely together through subject associations and organizations like the PTI to ensure that such new curricula reflect the most significant and up-to-date 'powerful' knowledge. The teacher's role is to provide all their pupils access to this, enable them to make sense of the world. Those subject networks will also need to persuade governments and the general public that teachers have the professional standards to take back control of the curriculum and its assessment, either through a college of teaching or a similar initiative. At the time of writing the Coalition government is displaying some schizophrenia about the extent of the curricular autonomy it is prepared to allow to schools but, nonetheless, there are now better opportunities for intelligent teacher-led curriculum development than at any time since 1988.

6

Curriculum leadership and the knowledge-led school

Carolyn Roberts

My context as a headteacher (2001–13)

I had no sooner taken a nervous first breath as a headteacher in 2001 when the Education Act (2002) set about revising the National Curriculum (NC) based on the principle that maintained schools should provide a balanced and broadly based curriculum that:

- *promotes the spiritual, moral, cultural, mental and physical development of learners at the school and within society and*

- *prepares learners at the school for the opportunities, responsibilities and experiences of adult life.*

The curriculum framework sought to guarantee an entitlement for learners of all backgrounds to standards, continuity and coherence and which would aid public understanding. It should instil in children a positive disposition to learning and a commitment to learn and promote and pass on essential knowledge, skills and understanding valued by society to the next generation.

The NC was still detailed and prescriptive at both Key Stages 3 and 4, but in 2005 Key Stage 3 was reviewed to allow schools to 'personalize' learning, a theme taken up by HMCI Christine Gilbert's '20–20 Vision' document in 2006. In 2008 the whole NC was reviewed again. Reviewer Mick Waters' set the tone:

> The curriculum should be treasured. There should be real pride in our curriculum; the learning that the nation has decided to set before its young. Teachers, parents, employers, the media and the public should all see the curriculum as something to embrace, support and celebrate. Most of all, young people should relish the opportunity for discovery and achievement that the curriculum offers.

After review the NC was gargantuan in reach. It had Aims:

> Education influences and reflects the values of society, and the kind of society we want to be. It is important, therefore, to recognise a broad set of common purposes, values and aims that underpin the school curriculum and the work of schools. Clear aims that focus on the qualities and skills learners need to succeed in school and beyond should be the starting point for the curriculum.

and slightly clearer Values:

> Education should reflect the enduring values that contribute to personal development and equality of opportunity for all, a healthy and just democracy, a productive economy, and sustainable development.

Further Values related to *the self, relationships, the diversity in our society and the environment. It was a* 'Curriculum for the Future'[1], set to

- raise achievement in all subjects, particularly in English and mathematics

- equip learners with the personal, learning and thinking skills they will need to succeed in education, life and work

- motivate and engages learners

- enable a smooth progression from primary, through secondary and beyond

- encourage more young people to go on to further and higher education

- give schools the flexibility to tailor learning to individual and local needs

- ensure that assessment supports effective teaching and learning

- provide more opportunities for focused support and challenge where needed.

Further inclusions were personal development, Every Child Matters imperatives, functional skills and personal, learning and thinking skills. These 'PLTS' were designed to produce independent enquirers, creative thinkers, reflective learners, team workers, self-managers

---

[1]There are various sources for the material presented here, which since the change of government in 2010 and the subsequent abolition of QCDA are now remarkably difficult to find. A good starting point however is www.teachfind.com for readers who may wish to track down the various discussion documents leading to the 2008 NC.

and effective participants. All these alongside 'cross-curricular dimensions' of identity and cultural diversity, healthy lifestyles, community participation, enterprise, global dimension and sustainable development, technology and the media, creativity and critical thinking, language, ICT and health and safety across the curriculum. Schools were pointed in the direction of competency frameworks and skills taxonomies promoted through other initiatives such as social and emotional aspects of learning (SEAL), RSA *Opening Minds* and Futurelab's *Enquiring Minds*.

Headteachers, perhaps not to be trusted to think for themselves, could engage in 'developing your curriculum'. It is worth looking at this instruction in full to demonstrate the expected limits of headteachers' independence:

The new secondary curriculum offers schools a real opportunity to innovate, building on existing good practice. To make the most of the opportunities offered by the new secondary curriculum, schools will need to reflect on their current curriculum.

- *What are its strengths and what needs to be developed?*

- *How well does it meet the wider aims of the curriculum?*

- *Does it reflect local contexts and meet the needs, interests and aspirations of all learners?*

- *How might you develop your curriculum to improve motivation and engagement and raise standards?*

- *Are there assumptions about how you use time, resources and approaches to planning that could helpfully be challenged or improved?*

The activities on the NC website[2] are designed to support thinking and discussion. The schools that piloted these materials found them useful in providing an evaluation of the strengths of their existing curriculum, and in identifying priorities for future development. To help schools implement and develop the new curriculum, a programme of support is available for headteachers, curriculum planners and subject leaders.

A change of government in 2010, however, brought further review, the outcomes of which we are just beginning to see. A DfE (2011) advisory committee and expert panel made up of 'top teachers, academics and business representatives' were set up to advise Michael Gove,

> To replace the current substandard curriculum with one based on the best school systems in the world, providing a world-class resource for teachers and children, consider what subjects should be compulsory at what age and consider what children should be taught in the main subjects at what age.

So that a new curriculum would

- embody rigour and high standards and create coherence
- ensure all children have the opportunity to acquire a core of essential knowledge in the key subject disciplines
- allow teachers the freedom to use their professionalism and expertise to help all children realize their potential

---

[2]This 'support and development' website is of course no longer available.

- give teachers greater professional freedom over how they organize and teach the curriculum

- develop a National Curriculum that acts as a benchmark for all schools and provides young people with the knowledge they need to move confidently and successfully through their education, taking into account the needs of different groups including the most able and pupils with special educational needs and disabilities (SEND)

- ensure the content of our National Curriculum compares favourably with the most successful international curricula in the highest performing jurisdictions, reflecting the best collective wisdom we have about how children learn and what they should know

- set rigorous requirements for pupil attainment that measure up to those in the highest performing jurisdictions in the world

- enable parents to understand what their children should be learning throughout their school career and therefore to support their education.

For headteachers of my generation the nightmare vision of control foreseen by Martin Roberts (Chapter 5) has been our reality. Trained on NPQH to be the Department's ground troops we might be forgiven for resigning ourselves to the delivery of an evermore tightly calibrated set of objectives where the NC, performance tables and Ofsted have defined our professional lives. Are they also capable of defining the curriculum, or should we be able to do that for ourselves?

What is the curriculum?

Heads talk about the curriculum a lot. We talk about structure and possibilities, flexible pathways and responsive setting, collapsed timetables and extended days: the hallmarks of 'innovation'. It is the structure and direction of the school day, the detail that a gifted deputy thinks up on the back of an old envelope or a powerful laptop. Courses on this are expensive and oversubscribed and children have benefited immeasurably from timetables then described as 'personalized'.

The personalized curriculum shibboleth has a shadow side for children and their learning. A school may offer six pathways at GCSE but only allow a child to choose one or two of them, where the child can most reliably reach C grades. The argument is simple: by channelling the child thus her chance of C grades is maximized, as is her access to the next stage of education. In pre-Wolf years, these pathways often included 'equivalent' courses of debatable value. As Wolf pointed out in her 2011 Report,

> performance measures combined with indiscriminate 'equivalencies' created perverse 'incentives' for schools, resulting in young people taking substandard courses that did not serve them well.

Some schools aimed for and achieved 100 per cent A*-C equivalent grades, and prospered by selling curriculum models to other schools: heads were knighted for such. That such courses and pathways, about which some children were given no choice at all, were useful for the school's performance but not the child's future demonstrates the perversity of the incentive and the desperation generated by high-stakes crude accountability.

And so traditional subjects declined. Only 25 per cent of students in state schools had grade C or above in a language in 2009, yet success percentages were quite high: schools only offered languages to top students. A similar pattern emerged with history and, to a lesser extent, geography.

Of course most schools behaved with perfect integrity, agonizing over curricula and making bold choices. The deregulation of Key Stage 3 allowed schools to decide its length, giving them freedom to move away from the NC diet. The RSA *Opening Minds* curriculum is a popular example of this, adopted by many successful or ambitious schools for laudable reasons, encouraged by exhortations such as the following (www.rsaopeningminds.org.uk).

RSA Opening Minds promotes innovative and integrated ways of thinking about education and the curriculum. Teachers design and develop a curriculum for their own schools based round the development of five key competences:

> *Citizenship*
> *Learning*
> *Managing Information*
> *Relating to people*
> *Managing Situations*

A competence based approach enables students not just to acquire subject knowledge but to understand, use and apply it within the context of their wider learning and life. It also offers students a more holistic and coherent way of learning which allows them to make connections and apply knowledge across different subject areas.

Such aims are also laudable and schools have a duty to ensure that children are reasonably adept at them before leaving school. But a good English teacher using *Of Mice and Men* or *Pride and Prejudice* will cover all of those competences – as would a study of Rio de Janeiro, the English Civil War or Islam. We are human and we live in society: we cannot avoid them. What our children need is the evidence of the best thinking or the worst mistakes of the past, so that they may step back from their experience and use knowledge to empower their future. Competences follow knowledge where teaching is expert. Does this define a good education?

What is a 'good' education?

This discussion is hard to have. It is polarized, swinging around iconic statements of knowledge and skills, 'vocational' and 'elite' education. It is deliberately confused with an older debate. Mention the primacy of subject knowledge and the importance of access for all to 'the best that has been thought and said' and risible battle lines are drawn. (This is what we talk about when we talk about grammar schools. Despite the evidence that *'academic selection entrenches advantage, it does not spread it'*, it has a siren call to the right. Selection is socially corrupted: in a society where the educational advantage of a middle-class child is clear by the age of 3, a test at 11 tests parental ambition and class aspiration, not ability and certainly not potential. It is teachers who make a difference, not selection tests.)

It is a version of this debate which surrounded the invention of the English Baccalaureate. Infuriated by the imposition of a new accountability measure heads set out to resist and ridicule the EBacc in a debate both bitter and entrenched. Schools accused the Secretary of State of trying to catch them out, judging them against unreasonable measures. Humanities and languages aspects of the six-subject EBacc were characterized as narrow minority interests, too challenging for most children to achieve C grade and very damaging to schools whose success was based on gaming the tables with 'skills-based' GCSE equivalences.

Curriculum choice

Further to understand a debate characterized in terms of knowledge versus skills we need to look at the curriculum choices schools make and why they make them. Schools which offer highly vocational Key Stage 4 courses argue that many young people, particularly those from challenging backgrounds, cannot see the purpose of education. They need to be persuaded of its utility through opportunities which build upon their experiences and prepare them for the workplace. This will make them enthusiastic, forward-thinking and compliant, improving both behaviour and life chances. Further, they need to be equipped with workplace skills which will give them a better chance in the employment market, such as entry-level hair and beauty (Salon Skills), basic mechanics (Motor Vehicle Skills) or 'personal effectiveness', 'life skills' or 'study skills'.

Tim Oates accurately described this conflation of motivation and curriculum as a category error. Liz Atkins' submission to Wolf (2001: 109) makes the point clearly:

If young people are disaffected, perhaps schools could explore methods of pedagogy rather than subjects – it is difficult to see how a person could be disengaged from the whole of a broad subject curriculum. . . . I am increasingly of the opinion that vocational education needs to be grounded in a broader, academic education so that young people have the necessary Basic Skills to progress freely.

So some schools use 'vocational' curricula (upon which many built performance table success) as the only way to keep children motivated or prevent them from literally life-threateningly becoming NEET. The evidence of the Wolf Report 2011 does not support this: disaffected children did not improve their attainment on vocational courses and were just as likely to drop out at 16+. Wolf's view is that vocational specialism at Key Stage 4 is risky and premature and the report seeks to restrict such courses to 20 per cent of curriculum time, 80 per cent being spent on traditional subject courses which develop and reinforce basic skills.

Good behaviour, rightly equated with motivation, is not predicated upon curriculum content. It is a prerequisite for student achievement but founded upon interesting and stimulating teaching, strong relationships between knowledgeable teachers and their classes and robust structures in schools. It is as possible in GCSE Spanish as it is in Life Skills, and the Spanish student will be having her horizons broadened. Adolescents are challenged by the drama of their own existence: they do not need pseudo-relevant curriculum content to reflect on their lives (which they do incessantly), but knowledge which will open doors to them, to academic excellence and social justice.

Academic excellence and social justice

Academic excellence is deceptive and schools need to try very hard not to build that on the shifting sands of 'good exam results'. 'Good exam results' depends on your measuring device.

Academic excellence means that young people are exposed to and know for themselves the best that has been thought and said. It develops young people's knowledge and understanding, for the good of themselves and society, as vital to the individual and the nation as good health. Academic excellence requires exacting recruitment of teachers of intellectual quality, expert knowledge, superb pedagogy, institutional stability, serious professionalism, constant resilience and healthy scepticism. It is based on the Nolan principles of selflessness, honesty, objectivity, openness, leadership, integrity and accountability. It is part of our commitment to the individual and collective worth of every child we serve.

Social justice follows naturally. Admission to a school committed to academic excellence is the right of each child independent of background, apparent ability or family wealth. Education for all should confer the benefits associated with education for the rich. So, if our national life values a particular kind of education such that those who have it are enabled to monopolize the most prestigious positions in society, then those educational doors must also be open to the children of the majority. How can it be the case that the education of 93 per cent of the nation's children leaves them unable to compete with 7 per cent educated privately? Social justice demands that we address this explicitly.

Social justice might also demand that we assault some of the other barriers to educational success faced by young people: poverty, exploitation, low aspiration, poor parenting, ill-health, bad housing, economic exploitation and unreasonable levels of responsibility. Educational success, however, is the single passport to prosperity and long life so nothing may be allowed to subvert it. It is not that schools should compensate for other problems or dilute their aims to make success easier, but that they must try to enable success in life through good education. It is the door to a better life. How can we make sense of this in school when so many other messages threaten to deafen us?

A different set of aims: Durham Johnston

Academic excellence is our first priority. We work so that all our young people have the best education we can provide. We want Johnstonians to be confident and articulate, determined to succeed and motivated to take responsibility for their own learning. We want them to value learning for itself, not just as the means to an end.

Taking our responsibility as public servants very seriously, we seek to offer the benefits and advantages that confer success and prosperity by imparting knowledge and habits of mind to last a lifetime. We do not close doors to any child, but enable them all to have access to powerful knowledge and deep subject learning. We educate our young people with excellence and equity so that they may feel at ease in the world, ready for hard work and global citizenship.

> *A commitment to social justice characterizes this comprehensive school. We work so that background is irrelevant to achievement and that aspiration is not limited by circumstance of birth. We want Johnstonians to be self-confident, reflective, inquiring, tolerant, positive and respectful of the needs of others. We give opportunities for leadership, cultural encounter and active citizenship.*
>
> *We aim for our school to be a sustainable, just and happy community so that our students understand how each person may be of value to society. Adults and young people alike share an ethic of hard work and public service. We want to be central to the life of Durham City and an educational force in the life of the communities we serve.*

These are the paradigm statements of Durham Johnston's school plan. We are an 11–18 mixed community comprehensive set amidst the beauty and deprivation of Durham City. A 1,550 students come from a wide range of socio-economic and educational backgrounds. We teach a traditional curriculum at Key Stages 3 and 4, and have an oversubscribed sixth form 97 per cent of whom go on to competitive university courses.

After first headship in a rebranded CE school in a very deprived area I returned to Johnston, a school I knew well in 2005. We are a confident, successful and oversubscribed school with a national reputation at A level. Our practice focuses on high-quality knowledge and making sure our young people achieve in demanding subjects including languages for all. Our Key Stage 4 curriculum adjusts every year to give pupils access to as many traditional subjects as possible. This fine tuning makes it easier each year for each pupil to study (on top of English, literature, maths, a language, RE and PE) two or three sciences and history or geography. Does this curriculum make us a good school?

Johnston is far from perfect. It is, however, to use Brian Lightman's term, a confident school so we are able to develop our curriculum calmly. Therefore, the adjunct to the school plan paradigms at the head of this chapter is our curriculum statement:

We have very high aspirations for all our young people and a close targeted, classroom, child-level focus on each student reaching a personal best based on a traditional liberal arts and sciences broad and balanced entitlement curriculum. We are constantly designing and redesigning a curriculum to fit each child's needs at all stages and levels, such as the focus group for lower attainers in years 7 and 8 and our 4-pathway KS4 curriculum. Extension work for the most able children is available through the Gifted and Talented programme.

We offer an easily-understandable and straightforward curriculum at Johnston preserving traditional subject divisions and finding the most interesting ways of teaching them. We do this so that the pathway to the most competitive courses and jobs is kept open for as many of our students as possible for as long as possible. We make it possible for them (rightly) to change their minds about their futures and still have quality qualifications for the next stage in life. For some students this will mean some time spent on rigorously planned and taught vocational courses. Where we cannot offer these ourselves, we work in partnership with other schools.

Our commitment to the best for all our students is demonstrated not only by our determination to give them the same levers as children whose parents pay for education outside the state sector, but by our close attention to equity. We are committed to making sure that young people from all of our widely-ranging socio-economic communities have the same opportunities and are encouraged to have the same ambitions. Nowhere is this more obvious than in our commitment to languages at Johnston in an era when only 25% of state school students achieve a GCSE language grade C or above in a foreign language while nearly 100% of independent school students do. We aim for our children to be able to compete in a global marketplace.

The better to test our commitment we seek to analyse our curriculum and all of our activities by postcode. This way we will know whether everything we offer reaches all of our communities.

We believe that our young people are encouraged to be articulate and confident, ready to take their places in the world alongside the best of their generation. Visitors and those who newly or infrequently meet them remind us that they are friendly and confident, talkative and searching.

Despite rhetorical flourishes this is not difficult stuff. It is the reliable curriculum of a reliable school, tweaked every year to improve opportunities. We believe that it helps us try to achieve remarkable things alongside our two main aims: high aspirations, a broad and balanced education, confident young people.

The knowledge-driven school

But we believe more than this. We are challenged by our place in the world as educators and want to see more than measurable outcomes.

So, we are considering 10 principles at Johnston this year as we work to move towards a thorough overhaul of our curriculum at classroom level.

1 Knowledge is worthwhile in itself.

Tell children this unapologetically: learning is the purpose of adolescence.

2 Schools transmit shared and powerful knowledge on behalf of society.

We teach what they need to make sense of and improve the world.

3 Shared and powerful knowledge is verified through learned communities.

We are model learners, in touch with research and subject associations.

4 Children need powerful knowledge to understand and interpret the world.

Without it they remain dependent upon those who have it or misuse it.

5 Powerful knowledge is cognitively superior to that needed for daily life.

It transcends and liberates children from their daily experience.

6 Shared and powerful knowledge enables children to grow into useful citizens.

As adults they can understand, cooperate and shape the world together.

7 Shared knowledge is a foundation for a just and sustainable democracy.

Citizens educated together share an understanding of the common good.

8 It is fair and just that all children should have access to this knowledge.

Powerful knowledge opens doors: it must be available to all children.

9 Accepted adult authority is required for shared knowledge transmission.

The teacher's authority to transmit knowledge is given and valued by society.

10 Pedagogy links adult authority, powerful knowledge and its transmission.

We need quality professionals to achieve all this for all our children.

It is in this context that our conviction about subject knowledge must be understood. All our children must be enabled to understand something of the world and the scope and reach of human endeavour so that they may create their futures. They will learn any amount of competencies as part of this undertaking, not least that there is much to know, and that learning is only starting as they leave school. If we are really skilled, they will also leave with a burning curiosity to know more, an understanding of how knowledge works, which subjects engage them and how to uncover the truth.

This is as necessary for Sam going to Oxford as Shannon heading for the FE college. Sam won't get within a mile of Oxford without it, and Shannon shouldn't have her life wasted relearning basic skills that she didn't get in school because her curriculum was made up of Personal Effectiveness and Learning to Learn. Sam's Extended Project in the sixth form was on Bach, not vital to his place to read Natural Sciences. Shannon does not need to know about Churchill to train to be a care home assistant, but her understanding of the world was enriched by a history teacher who knew some really interesting stuff, and she can write precise and grammatical care reports. They are both empowered and enabled by subject knowledge.

The future is Future 3: Knowledge and the curriculum

In May 2008, I was early for a meeting in Senate House and, persuaded by my son's need of a debit card in Waterstone, I wandered into Education and chanced upon Michael's *Bringing Knowledge Back In*. The rest of that year found me on daily lunch duty sitting on a step at the back of the gym confounding smokers and reading a densely argued, compelling plea for a sensible approach to the curriculum in our schools.

What none of this chapter covers is the actual, taught curriculum. Inside the units of time of the school day what are children learning? What do they know as a result of the time spent in class? What is it that constitutes solid learning in history, or maths? What is it in the science or English curriculum that builds a foundation for the next step? When the revised NC offers its brief list of concepts, how should schools decide what to teach?

Johnstonians until 2002 had a quaint experience in Year 7 geography dissecting the layout of a pit village, despite mining ending 30 years earlier. Keeping up to date with one's subject 20 years after graduation requires active engagement with the subject which must be both required and facilitated by schools. This is central to Young's Future 3: knowledge as defined by subjects is the central activity of the good school of the future, equipping the child with what she needs to begin to make her way in the world. Everything else follows that.

Conclusion

It is a privileged child indeed who can guarantee that home will be a sufficient foundation for his knowledge of the world. The most enlightened homes are products of their time: it is the next generation of parents, for example, who will understand how to regulate the effects of social networking on young teenagers. The least offer restricted hopes and aspirations. If we do not teach the best that has been thought and said, the knowledge and skills of science and mathematics, the way the world works in history and geography and the consolations of literature and music then we leave children to the lottery of their birth and widening social injustice. The middle-class child of graduate parents will learn from the dinner table between cello lessons, the church youth group and the local harriers: children of the debilitatingly poor or disorganized will not. Unless we can alter this, what are schools for?

7

Subject teachers in knowledge-led schools

David Lambert

This chapter is written by a former secondary school geography teacher and head of department. I have written it to show why subject specialist teachers should be excited by a 'knowledge turn' in schools. I argue that teachers can take back professional responsibility for 'curriculum making' following the introduction of a revised National Curriculum in 2014, which will according to the government be 'knowledge led'. There is now an opportunity for teachers to engage with knowledge in a manner that has not been a priority in schools for the best part of 20 years – ironically since the introduction of a national curriculum in England in 1991.

This is emphatically not out of some fuddy-duddy search for the comfort to be found in standard textbooks or behind closed classroom doors, and nor is it some misty-eyed yearning for a simpler, golden past. It arises from a fundamental progressive instinct shared by many if not all teachers, that their work with children and young people should aspire to create educational encounters of significance: that is, lessons that are worthwhile, enjoyable, challenging and motivating.

I have always wanted to wake pupils up intellectually, help open their eyes and equip them with knowledge about how the world 'works'. To do this we need disciplinary resources and my chosen resource was geography. Thus, when I found myself as a deputy head after a decade or so teaching I made a choice – in order that I could continue to work principally with the two big ideas that were consuming my interest: geography and education. I became a university based teacher educator (and for ten years chief executive of the Geographical Association). This chapter therefore also takes in matters of teacher preparation, support and development.

Throughout this book we have been acutely aware that many teachers find it less than comfortable to talk about knowledge, lest it betrays them as traditionalists fixed in what we call a Futures 1 vision of their work and lacking in creativity and relevance. This often rests on a restricted conception of knowledge, where it is taken to mean superficial facts, resulting in excruciating efforts to distinguish knowledge from understanding – to put 'knowledge' in its place as it were, and to distance teaching from Hirschian lists and rote learning (Hirsch, 1987; 2007).

However, to downplay knowledge in order to prize understanding is, as we noted in Chapter 1, a professional distraction when we know well that we cannot have knowledge without understanding, just as we cannot have understanding without knowledge. It is a distraction that can, if we are reluctant to do the hard and inconvenient thinking about what knowledge we would like children to acquire and develop through their school life, result in a carefree – or careless – attitude, as if knowledge simply did not matter or could be taken for granted (for free from the internet). Indeed, in some outcomes-based curricula it really does not seem to matter. This is where the content of lessons is driven by what is thought to be of interest to the children and where *learning as a process* becomes fetishized; by which I mean learn*ing* becomes the product of school, not what is learn*ed* – and an end, rather than a means to an end. We then talk about learning at the expense of what is learned, which if we are honest is a profound abrogation of responsibility which certainly undermines teaching and teachers.

This chapter is written from a subject teacher's perspective, not defensively in an attempt to protect hallowed traditions or curriculum territories, but openly and expansively in a manner that holds to the emancipatory ideals encapsulated by the notion 'education for all'. The discussion is therefore grounded in a deep concern for what it means to be a teacher. We shall focus mainly on the secondary school curriculum, and reflect particularly on some implications of re-engaging with a knowledge-led curriculum for teacher preparation and ongoing professional support. Subject teachers are often isolated, often bombarded by cost-efficient CPD on generic themes such as learning to learn and assessment for learning. What this chapter will show is that the re-engagement of teachers with knowledge almost certainly requires strengthening subject specialist teaching communities beyond the individual school. Specialist subject teachers need to explore the relationships between the school subject (aligned to educational goals and purposes) and the wider academic discipline (aligned to research and knowledge creation).

These relationships are not straightforward and are difficult to engineer. The second half of this chapter takes a more detailed look at one subject in particular – geography – as an illustrative case study. I fully realize that what I have to say here may not translate easily to other subjects. In a way that is one of the points we wish to emphasize in this book, that the subjects are different and that this is both the strength and the challenge of a subject-based curriculum. The boundaries between subjects are important (this is not to say they cannot be crossed). Their traditions are different, resulting from and producing different expertise and giving both teachers and learners particular identities. We will illustrate this through geography. We hope that teachers, researchers and teacher educators across the disciplines will be able to explore a Future 3 approach to the school curriculum through a full range of subjects.

Subjects, powerful knowledge and pedagogic rights

The problem addressed initially in Chapter 4 and explored further here is how to express a progressive case for subjects as the basis for the curriculum when so many see them as backward looking. Our priority is that *all* students are given the opportunity to acquire knowledge and refine their understanding so that it will become a resource for them even after they leave school. We emphasize subjects because they embody the purpose of schools in taking students *beyond* their everyday experience. Furthermore, subjects provide boundaries and hence a sense of identity for teachers and learners and collective resource for teachers, for example, through subject associations.

This chapter seeks to describe an expansive and convincing view of subjects in the school curriculum fit for this day and age. We do this in a way that resists the reductive tendencies present in both more 'traditionalist' and 'progressive' education discourses which hollow out education and its true potential to enable people to imagine alternative futures. This results either from a fixed and restricted concept of 'given' knowledge, albeit sometimes dressed up in classic Arnoldian terms of 'best of what is thought and written', or from a rejection of the efficacy of subjects themselves in favour of generic skills and competences, often grounded in the 'relevance' of the everyday.

We argue, with the Russian psychologist Lev Vygotsky, that truly educational encounters set us apart from day-to-day experiences to enable us, after the British sociologist Basil Bernstein, to think the 'not yet thought' (Bernstein, 2000: 30), a formulation that works both for the individuals and for societies. Bernstein did not dismiss the everyday, but saw that it is the very interchange between expert or disciplinary discourses and 'common-sense' or everyday knowledge that is pedagogically powerful.

It can be argued, correctly, that universities and schools have quite a different function when it comes to knowledge. Universities are both in the knowledge-producing business (research) and in taking students, some of whom will be researchers, to the leading edge of their disciplines and in so doing inducting young people into the procedures and methods of the discipline. Schools however have a different relation to knowledge: they do not produce knowledge, but they do transfer and communicate it. This no longer means that students are simply expected to listen, take notes and regurgitate, activities that only a minority are any good at. Teachers encourage their students to enquire and investigate. In doing so students use and manipulate data to draw and then test conclusions, and they debate and learn how to argue. Indeed, the important pedagogic advances of recent decades, contributing to our understanding of the strength of active or 'constructivist' pedagogic strategies (see Roberts, 2003; 2013) may have blurred somewhat the distinction between knowledge creation or development (in the universities) and knowledge acquisition and development in schools. Although students may be engaged in what is frequently referred to as 'knowledge construction' in the geography classroom, what they are really doing is 'making meaning' for themselves. This is extremely important, but only very rarely does it result in 'new knowledge' that challenges leading edge research. Making meaning may result in knowledge that is new to the individual, but it is not necessarily new to the wider subject community or from the perspective of specialist researchers. The distinction being made here is important for two reasons.

First, it raises a question about the relationship between school subjects and university-based research disciplines. Elements of the constellations of knowledge produced by the disciplines are drawn on in many sectors of society, for example, by the professions like medicine and engineering where it is well known that the close relationship exists between research universities and hospitals, transnational business and start-up companies. The relationship is direct and symbiotic. Time was when this was also true for school subjects, when the selection of knowledge was primarily the responsibility of examination boards employing university specialists as chief examiners and who were often prominent and influential in subject associations. University academics also wrote school textbooks. However, this has not been the case for at least a generation. Not only have academics become increasingly specialized within their disciplinary fields, but pedagogic matters have come to dominate education discourse (child centredness has replaced subject-centred teaching) and school curriculum matters have become increasingly bureaucratized in a manner that excludes university academics. Since roughly the 1980s educationists in various guises as teachers, teacher educators, advisers and consultants have become the dominant influence in national curriculum formulation and until very recently GCSE and A level specifications too. It is not coincidental that during this period the leadership of the main subject associations was also less clearly in the hands of academics from the disciplines.

If the university discipline takes the lead – or at least has an influential voice – in the selection of the knowledge contents of school subjects then teachers have an obligation to 'keep up' with discoveries and developments in the discipline (suggesting a highly significant role for subject associations).[1] This is far less the case when the subject is deemed less relevant than pedagogic experience; in truth, if teachers are not obliged to 'keep up' as

---

[1] Although not strictly relevant to the present discussion, it is interesting to note that in the United Kingdom school geography predated geography as a university discipline. Geography departments were set up at the beginning of the twentieth century (Oxford was the first during the last decade of the nineteenth century) principally to supply graduates to teach geography in the newly established state-funded secondary school system. Of course, once established university departments went on to develop the discipline conceptually and theoretically in ways that were not guided by the existing school curriculum.

new knowledge is developed then what is the purpose of school subjects and of subject specialist teachers? These are particularly interesting questions that possibly play differently in different subject areas. For an unruly discipline such as geography can appear to be, these questions are very tricky, for it has (as with the other social sciences) relatively little of what Bernstein calls 'verticality' unlike mathematics or the sciences. However, if there is no easily agreed lineage between secondary school geography and what is being taught and learned closer to the research frontier, how can geography prepare students for undergraduate subjects and a possible research future? Moreover, how can we be sure teachers are engaging all children with the state of the art of thought and practice in the discipline? After all, advances in the discipline are important to grasp, for we can then see how geographical perspectives in the past have been misleading – or even downright harmful as in the uncritical adoption of theoretical perspectives such as environmental determinism.[2]

The second problem relates closely to the first. It is to do with locus of power and control of the curriculum. This book argues that the curriculum should foreground knowledge. At its simplest, for example, in the case of the reformed National Curriculum in England where the 'core of essential knowledge' in geography for children from ages 5–14 years is now itemized on just four pages (see Lambert and Hopkin, 2014), the curriculum frames what counts as

---

[2]Put simply, the idea that environmental circumstances such as climate have a direct bearing on human inventiveness and productivity, leads to flawed but convenient conclusions about the 'superiority' of the temperate latitudes and its peoples over the tropics.

valid – or at least the authorized – knowledge to be taught and learned in schools. Even so, the formalized curriculum, especially when it is as brief as in the case of England, is a statement of intent or a set of guidelines only. It offers no guarantees over what is actually taught and learned in schools. This is why it is important to distinguish between a National Curriculum and the curriculum of individual schools.

I conclude from the discussion so far that there is a serious 'curriculum problem' in schools which we describe as a curriculum *making* issue (as distinct from a design or planning issue). The geography curriculum *as it is implemented by teachers and experienced by students* is always open to interpretation which is why we do need specialist trained teachers – teachers who are able to interpret the official intentions laid down in statute through the lens of their specialist knowledge, for it is this that provides the subject curriculum with its educational potential. It is for this reason that I find the idea of 'powerful knowledge' helpful.

Powerful knowledge

In his fifth and final volume of *Class, Codes and Control* (Bernstein, 2000) introduced the idea of the 'pedagogic rights' of young people to individual enhancement, social inclusion and political participation. These 'rights' are expressed as outcomes of educational processes. For Bernstein, access to knowledge is the key educational contribution to fighting the inequalities that are implicit in his identification of pedagogic rights. This provides a context for Michael Young's (a former student and colleague of Bernstein's) concept of 'powerful knowledge' discussed in Chapter 3. In direct opposition to those who urge a skills-based curriculum based on the development of generic 'competences' (often deemed especially appropriate to 'less academic' students), Young argues that it is a matter of social equity that all young people have the right of access to 'powerful' – or disciplinary – knowledge. This argument, which we have developed in various ways throughout this book, counters both the relativism of much 'progressive' skills-led educational thinking and its corollary that the curriculum should be based on pupil's interests (referred to in this book as Future 2), and the inadequacies of 'traditionalist' views which see the contents of the school curriculum as a largely fixed selection of 'core knowledge' (Hirsch, 1987; 2007) which we characterize as Future 1. Powerful knowledge[3] emphasizes intellectual resources which are difficult to identify from a Hirschian list of core knowledge.

Our hunch is that it is helpful to express school subject knowledge as 'powerful knowledge' as conceptually it counters the inadequacies of both traditionalist (Future 1) and generic progressive (Future 2) educational thought. It firms up the notion

---

[3]The following list is an abridged and revised list (Young, 2009) from an earlier attempt to define 'powerful knowledge':
- It is abstract and theoretical (conceptual) – it is concerned with the general not the particular
- the concepts associated with it are interrelated – they are part of a system
- it is reliable, but open to challenge
- it is often counter-intuitive to experience – we do not experience our world going round the sun;
- it has a reality that is independent of the direct experience of the teacher and the learner – we do not experience society or gravity but we know they are real if we break their rules.

of children's pedagogic rights: it forms a rationale for progressive educational thought that is knowledge oriented.

Teachers as curriculum leaders

An interesting question arises at this point: who 'owns' (say) *geographical* powerful knowledge? And, can it be specified, for example, through national standards and curricula? National jurisdictions around the world have attempted to lay down the 'standards' for the school curriculum, including its geographical component. But in most cases, we argue, practitioners are conscious of the limits of such instruments. They are blunt and often fail to take account the nuances of context.

In the context of this discussion it is clear that a national curriculum for any subject – geography is an example – while useful, in itself achieves comparatively little on its own. The words on the page require interpretation and application by teachers to form a coherent teaching programme. Even if this work is mediated through the adoption of a textbook and is thus textbook-led, how the textbook is used will have significant impact on the curriculum as it is experienced by the students. This is partly through the various pedagogic techniques brought into play to assist students in 'reading' the text, partly through the relationship the teacher can build with the students as individuals and as a group but also partly resulting from the extent of the teacher's grasp of the subject matter. By the latter we mean a little more than 'the amount and organization of knowledge per se in the mind of the teacher, and something different from a technically sound 'pedagogic content knowledge' (Schulman, 1986: 9), important though these attributes are. We are alluding to the quality of the teacher's understanding of the subject's goals and purposes in the context of the discipline; that is, the potential and possibilities of geography contributing to the idea of students 'being educated'. We are referring to the clarity with which the teacher has grasped why the subject is worth teaching.

In this sense, we argue that *all* teachers are to some extent, 'curriculum makers'. The act of 'curriculum making' can be performed well and it can be done badly, but it cannot be avoided. In this book we argue that the concept of a Future 3 school provides a way to 'frame' its 'curriculum making' in fulfilling a school's broader educational goals.

What this section has set out to show is that young people have a pedagogic right to powerful subject-based knowledge as the best knowledge we have in a particular field. This places a significant responsibility on the shoulders of teachers that goes far beyond the requirement to demonstrate 'competence'. However, as subject specialists, they are not alone – they have the resources of their specialist subject community to draw on. It is this that supports their professional expertise and the trust that parents place in them. In the following sections, we examine these arguments more closely using geography as an illustrative case.

Whatever happened to geographical knowledge?

Of course, in themed lessons oriented by skills and competences, even in the most extreme Future 2 setting, students will be learning about something. Truly content free lessons are hard to envisage, and for this reason to argue for a knowledge-led school or curriculum appears to some as a somewhat superfluous, unnecessary claim. So why would we expend effort on bringing knowledge back in? It never went away.

The problem here is the confusion between knowledge and content. Many who advocate a skills-based curriculum, for example, emphasizing 'thinking skills' and/or 'learning power', often do so in the context of the loosely defined idea of the twenty-first-century 'knowledge society' with its enormous computing power and free and easy access to infinite quantities of information. It is remarkable watching young people operate smart phones and other gadgets with such remarkable dexterity that they can find answers to questions that arise in their daily lives almost instantly. Teachers cannot ignore this or pretend that digital technologies have not transformed some of our received understandings of education and how it functions. And why would they even want to ignore the wonderful affordances of technology? However, to imagine that almost instant access to several million references to whatever key word has been 'googled' equates with that user developing their knowledge – or worse, to imagine that their knowledge development is irrelevant now that information can be wirelessly channelled to us in infinite quantities – is confusing information skills with knowledge development.

I will illustrate this with a very simple example, of digitized mapping. Many of us now use satnav as a matter of course. Satnav devices are remarkable, a fabulous outcome of satellite technology providing cheap, accurate navigational assistance via your smart phone or at the switch of a button in your car. Why then should we teach 'maps' in geography lessons? It is interesting that this question does not arise in military training in the navy. Knowledge of pencil and paper navigation techniques are as important now as they have ever been, not least because satellite technology is useless when the equipment is damaged, or when the electricity is cut and the batteries are down. But more profoundly for us it is also based, ultimately on the realization that satellite navigation is not a reliable 'magic'. It does not just 'happen'. It is not just 'there'. Mercator's projection is underneath it, for reasons that make sense if you understand the principle purpose of Mercator's projection (which was, unlike more recent 'equal area' projections of the world map, designed to enable reliable navigation).

Maps of course are not simply designed to facilitate navigation: an enormously important industry has grown up based on geographic information science (GIS). This is where we can analyse layers of spatially located data such as where people live and the services they use – often captured by supermarket loyalty cards, credit card transactions, and so on – in a manner that can serve many purposes (including getting us to buy more). There is little doubt that children and young people should be exposed to, and use, GIS in school. However, no matter how powerful and dazzling its technology, GIS does not really replace 'mapwork' in school.

As GIS is becoming part of everyday experience, as with the satnav device, its use is in some respects unremarkable. Knowledge and understanding of what it is, why it has been developed and how it can be used is arguably more important to learn in school. As with maps, drawn to represent places, landscapes and spatial relationship over the centuries, we can learn about the power and the limits of

GIS. We might also marvel at the beauty of maps (and GIS images) and how they can lie and distort our viewpoint. Mapwork was never simply about practising skills. Mapwork can take us into the realm of imagination, of speculation, of propaganda, but anchored in the knowledge of rules and conventions and practices (geographers can fill in the details here – of grids, projections, symbols, isolines, choropleth, etc.). Specialist knowledge about maps and GIS is developed in geography lessons. Or put it this way: if it is not, then it probably is not developed anywhere else and the school student has no means of beginning to comprehend this aspect of 'everyday magic'. Their curiosity has not been pricked and their knowledge has not been developed beyond the everyday. It could be argued that anyone to whom this applies in this day and age is undereducated.

The purpose of this section is to acknowledge the truth that while geography lessons – pretty well all lessons – are usually about something, this does not absolve us of the responsibility to think hard about the knowledge being developed in geography lessons. This is not because lessons have become somehow 'content free', but because there may be serious doubts over how the lessons contribute to pupils' knowledge development, meaning conceptual development and the intellectual resources students acquire to help them make sense of the world. In all subjects, geography included, there is knowledge that can help them do this – and knowledge that is not so good. Students come to school with knowledge of all kinds, but at school they need to be exposed to better knowledge. This places great responsibility on teachers to make judgements about what to teach, judgements that cannot be left entirely to others, including as I hinted above to textbook writers.

It is perhaps salutary to explore this point in the context of several key and very influential texts in geography education in the latter years of the twentieth century. Each of these is emblematic of the 'curriculum thinking' which at the time (in the 1970s and 1980s) deliberately set out to make a response to the limits of a Futures 1 approach to schooling. Such curriculum thinking brought in psychological perspectives, theories of learning and to some extent social, environmental and other issues and concerns. Arguably these developments tended to displace knowledge – and the fundamental curriculum question (as distinct from more pedagogic concerns) which is 'what shall we teach?' These developments steadily put the school curriculum on a Future 2 trajectory. Thus, geography was consciously expressed not as an end in itself but as a 'medium of education' (Naish, 1997). Further examples are *Learning through Geography* (Slater, 1982) and *Thinking through Geography* (Leat, 1998). These influential texts appeared to reposition geography as a body of knowledge as a (mere) vehicle for 'learning'. To what extent do these formulations steer us away from the hard thinking we are advocating about what knowledge to teach in geography lessons? To be fair there is a lot of geography in Slater's fine book. However, there is very little by the time we get to Leat: subject knowledge has become almost incidental. The subject itself had been undermined, having become subservient to 'thinking skills'.

If geographical knowledge is undermined in the school curriculum, we can ask in what specific ways may we be weakening the educational outcomes of young people? This, as Roger Firth (2011) has shown, is to ask in what ways we diminish the educational experience for young people if we do not systematically induct them into ways of encountering the Earth as an object of thought, and what the study of geography has revealed to us through this effort.

On the need to be 'topical and relevant'

In a chapter exploring the nature of school geography in changing times, Charles Rawding probably speaks for many in urging that the subject, as expressed in school curriculum, should be up to date and 'relevant'. This is the basis for lamenting the National Curriculum in 1991 for 'imposing a more traditional geography curriculum' and for taking 'a distinct backwards step' (Rawding, 2013: 284). This sentiment leads Rawding to conclude, we think astonishingly, that under the theme of population geography, for example, the demographic transition model should be abandoned as 'old hat'.[4] It seems to me that although 'demographic transition' may not be inevitable and invariable, it is a powerful model that forms part of an architecture with which to think – and which can be modified and refined, extended and developed. In this sense it is powerful knowledge.

Other iconic figures and models are consigned to the waste bin with equal abandon, simply because they are old and deemed 'invalid' to the present day: landscape analysis derived from

---

[4]This describes the idealized transition in societies from a situation of high birth rates and high death rates to one of low birth rates and low death rates. As medical advances are embedded faster than social, economic and cultural changes that result in smaller families, low death rates often precede low birth rates causing a spike in population growth rates.

W. M. Davis is one such (Rawding, 2013: 287), despite a leading academic geographer, Tim Cresswell, recently commenting on his 'remarkable' contribution: 'one of the two or three most important people in the development of physical geography'[5] (Cresswell, 2013: 11). To brush this aside completely, mainly to allow for a more 'issues'-oriented physical geography, dominated one imagines by the impact of 'natural hazards', seems a little rash. It is in line of course with those who are drawn by topicality or relevance. The latter especially is a tricky idea, as it is commonly used unproblematically to mean 'immediacy' in the sense that the subject matter has ready meaning to children: and clearly, it is not easy to justify Davis's cycles of erosion on the grounds of everyday relevance! It is, however, somewhat reckless to ignore the disciplinary hinterland, the ideas and the figures who have contributed and the notion that our knowledge progresses, for in the end this undermines the notion of discipline itself (and therefore part of the case for the subject on the school curriculum). Just as we are not advocating teaching the demographic transition model as an objective, singular account that cannot be challenged or modified, the Davisian 'cycle of erosion' is not best taught as 'factual' representation to be proved right or wrong. But neither are we suggesting that because few if any researchers in physical geography attach much contemporary credence to Davis we therefore need to remove his ideas from the school curriculum,

---

[5]W. M. Davis was an American physical geographer working in the early years of the past century and enormously influential in his approach to landscape evolution, an approach to understanding landscape change that was superseded by a greater focus on process studies.

for as a pedagogic model, ideas such as 'cycles of erosion' remain powerful. It is as unhelpful in geography to assume that the only relevant knowledge is recent, as it is in English literature, science, mathematics or art. I acknowledge that non-recent ideas have a very different role in say physics and literature: for example, Newton is not studied as a figure in the same way as Shakespeare. But the question remains how to realize the potential of using school subjects to provide epistemic access to forms and fields of 'powerful knowledge'.

To counter these arguments many readers may wish to stress the claim that above all geography in schools is (or should be) about the contemporary world: that is, there is no time for the 'theories of the dead'. Now, we have much sympathy for geography's place in the school curriculum being justified in terms of its capacity to help students meet and comprehend contemporary events, issues and processes: it is good to see 'geography in the news' notice boards in schools. The mistake is to imagine that focusing only on our day-to-day experience of the world is the best way of understanding it, or geography. All school subjects – certainly, all those listed in the previous paragraph, and in addition history – claim their curriculum space in terms of understanding the world and our place in it today. Even the classics will do this. The curriculum question is to do with selecting the knowledge that exists outside the direct experience of the students and the teachers; that is, knowledge which has been created and developed by the wider disciplinary communities, which is worthwhile and relevant – relevant in the sense that it helps develop systematicity in our thinking plus a deepening and broadening of our perspectives. This knowledge is conceptual and in geography it often takes the form, as we have seen through my examples, of systems and models (which are sometimes called maps).

The line of thought taken in this section, which essentially challenges notions of relevance and topicality, finds some resonance with Tim Oates recommendations regarding the 2010–14 National Curriculum debates and subsequent revisions (Oates, 2010). He argued that it ought to be possible to think of the national curriculum as enduring and stable, and therefore not requiring modification too frequently. Frequent revision becomes necessary when the National Curriculum mistakenly specifies too much – including what he calls 'context' which is akin to the day-to-day setting, or in geography the case study.[6] Pedagogically, context matters as it can help create access, motivate interest and 'the need to know'. But in some ways it is ephemeral and the context one may choose to illustrate a concept or develop and idea may change, depending on events or even on the children one is teaching. Thus, Oates has asserted that a subject curriculum, stripped of context, may be as 'dry as dust' – as it is nothing more or less than a selection of that core of essential knowledge, expressed as substantive concepts, that the subject provides and which we need to teach.

Put like this, we heap enormous responsibilities onto teachers as curriculum makers (see further) and we can readily see why well prepared and knowledgeable subject specialist teachers are required to meet these responsibilities. The National Curriculum in itself need not be motivating or exciting: we cannot expect it to be for it

[6]In this sense in geography 'context' has a special significance, summed up in the well-known phrase, 'place matters' Understanding the significance of context is part of geography's 'powerful knowledge'.

is or should be simply a selection of essential contents (expressed as concepts – in geography examples include: weather and climate; cities; population migration). However teachers certainly do need to be interesting, engaging and occasionally exciting: They need to be able to provide motivating ways and means for students to access the curriculum. It is for this reason alone that the widely adopted delivery metaphor in teaching (we 'deliver' the National Curriculum) is so woefully inadequate. Curriculum making, as opposed to delivery, is a creative and highly disciplined activity which in effect melds curriculum and pedagogy. Thus teachers need to provide the means and space to engage students in order for them to make meaning.

This is in line with constructivist pedagogies, but it must not stop there. Students need also to ensure that their personal meanings are put against what is known, and how we know it. To do this teaching episodes and the resources selected for the lesson are in effect 'curricularized', not treated as ends in themselves or justified solely by fulfilling particular lesson objectives but as contributing to broader aims. It is likely that different subjects have different means at their disposal to do this. In history, for example, it appears that 'substantive concepts' such a 'revolution' or 'medieval' serve different purposes in guiding the development of pupils' historical perspectives and thoughts to second-order concepts such as causation, evidence, interpretation and change.

The fine art of 'curriculum making'

It will be clear from even a cursory reading of this chapter so far that we have a view about teachers as professionals that extends far beyond the idea of an educational technocrat. One way to interpret the arguments made here is to recognize that teachers need to do much deep and careful thinking before they even enter the classroom. This thinking revolves around the crucial curriculum question which is 'what shall I teach?' In a Future 3 school this question is unavoidably the responsibility of the teacher – supported of course by close colleagues, the leadership team in school and (this final point is vital) external networks including those that help maintain a productive and meaningful relationship with the wider discipline. The question is not answered, at least not fully, by the examination specification, syllabus – and least of all by the National Curriculum. All of these, especially the latter, need interpretation, elaboration and manipulation – for example, in deciding on the balance between breadth and depth, how to sequence ideas, the relationship between 'extensive' factual knowledge with more 'intensive' conceptual knowledge, the choice of context/exemplars, all these matters arise well before we even start to think about the structure of individual lessons and they are driven by a sense of overarching aims. Thus, lessons may be well structured by objectives, but curriculum thinking is characterized by goals and purposes.

Thus, in this section of the chapter we investigate the idea of 'curriculum making' as set out initially by the Geographical Association (GA) in its 'manifesto' of 2009 (GA, 2009). The term 'curriculum making' is familiar and has been used widely in geography teaching for at least a century. However, the GA has tried to specify its contemporary usage to describe a crucial aspect of teachers' work: that is, the intellectual and creative work alluded to earlier which in this book we refer to as Future 3. Although in this book we are making an important conceptual distinction between curriculum (primarily concerned with the knowledge contents) and pedagogy (mainly concerned with activity and learning processes), in describing curriculum making we are pointing to the practical melding of the two, as Figure 7.1 shows. We shall use a case study of the GAs thought leadership as a means to describe a 'possibilist' approach (Lambert and Hopkin, 2014) to developing the knowledge-led curriculum. By 'possibilist' we mean an approach (though not a set of rules and procedures) to interpreting the National Curriculum, or an examination specification, in a way that leads to a Future 3 'curriculum of engagement' rather than a Future 1 'curriculum of compliance' or delivery (see Chapter 2).

The GA's 2009 manifesto itself was a product of a particular set of circumstances, which resulted in a combination of

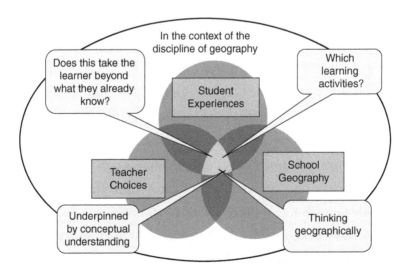

FIGURE 7.1 *Curriculum making for geography teachers.*

assumptions, policies and practices which we are calling Future 2. A new National Curriculum had been launched based on a vast, complicated curriculum model known as the 'big picture'. This summed up the state of the art curriculum thinking and took a distinctive focus provided by three innocuous aims: to create successful learners, confident individuals and responsible citizens. While it is not impossible to align geography (or any other subject) to these aims, the starting point of this curriculum design was clearly not 'what to teach'. It was instead the perceived 'needs' of the child in the context of twenty-first-century society, implied by the government's slogan Every Child Matters that heralded their concern for the 'personalization' of schooling. This is not the place to critique the 'big picture' in any detail: suffice to say that subjects were undermined under a complex set of whole school requirements of dimensions, themes and skills. Such an approach to 'grand curriculum design' is of course still argued for by its main advocate Mick Waters (2013).

For those of us who felt that geographical knowledge was important, the 2008 'big picture' needed to be challenged. The 'manifesto', under its title A Different View, made such a challenge and it can be explored in full at www.geography.org.uk/adifferentview. In sum, it was an attempt by the GA to make a strong and perhaps provocative statement about geography, expressed as a 'disciplinary resource', and an approach to education which was articulated partly through Richard Peters' concept of 'initiation' (1963) using his well-known position that to be educated is not so much to arrive at a destination, but to 'travel with a different view'. The manifesto, which took several forms including short videos designed to be used with students, in effect asked how geographical knowledge contributes to our being able to understand the world in new ways.

A fundamental component of the manifesto was 'curriculum making' which explicitly recognized the responsibility and the role of specialist teachers in working with the subject to create a 'curriculum of engagement'. In short, pedagogic competence and a respect for children's experiences and prior knowledge, though important, were not enough. The diagram (Figure 7.1) attempts to illustrate this.

The diagram is readily interpreted in terms of its self-evident invitation to work towards 'balance' in the midst of the competing priorities – to serve student needs, to demonstrate practical classroom knowledge and skill and to impart the knowledge contents. Of course, these categories are rarely as distinct from each other as this model implies. However, teaching that is too focused in any one of these domains risks being inadequate: for instance, if it is too child-centred it runs the risk of failing to move children beyond their everyday knowledge (F2), and too subject centred we run the risk of failing to enable all students access specialized disciplinary knowledge as we are insensitive to the need to provide opportunities for meaning making and possibly have a too fixed view of subject knowledge (F1). In this sense the model describes the practical act of curriculum making in terms of merging the conceptually distinct categories of curriculum and pedagogy (i.e. the 'what' and the 'how').

A more sophisticated reading of this model is also possible, one which recognizes that the intellectual and practical work that it implies takes place within a wider context of the disciplinary community (which also has its own socio-political context). In particular, this points to the relationship that exists between the school subject and the wider discipline which in geography is every bit as complex and problematic as it is in other subjects, whether in science, mathematics, history or the arts. It may be unreasonable to expect school teachers to read research literature emerging from highly specialized disciplinary communities, just as it is probably unrealistic to expect academics to have much more than a layperson's working knowledge of the school system. However, this is not to say that school science, or geography teachers should tolerate the kind of break with their disciplines that the 2008 National Curriculum implied. It is healthy to be sceptical about Futures 1 and 2 trends in education as noted in the previous section. Whereas the former take knowledge for granted, the latter can undermine the place of knowledge altogether. It is time to argue for better access to high-quality subject focused CPD, for to achieve a Future 3 school subject teachers carry much curriculum making responsibility.

Conclusion

I cannot teach glaciation to my pupils (in Whitechapel) because they will never encounter it. It is nothing to do with their lives and they do not see the relevance.

This is a quotation from a trainee teacher in an inner urban school (dated 4 March 2013). It is disturbing because it argues, perhaps inadvertently, for the removal of geography (and a whole lot more besides) from the curriculum. It also makes assumptions about the pupils which are almost certainly wrong (that they will never travel, for example, or that they cannot use their imaginations). In short, it reveals a very narrow conception of geography's contribution to the education of young people. It makes assumptions about 'relevance' explored earlier in this chapter. It may even imply an assumption that academic content in the curriculum has no place in an inner urban school in the east end of London. There is no doubt that teaching glaciation to young teenagers requires ingenuity, for there are abstract ideas (such as geological time) and other difficulties (such as conceptualizing the thickness and spatial extent of ice accumulations and its erosive power) to overcome. But the topic can inspire and enthral. And more to the point it can be the 'way in' to a deeper understanding of the following, for example:

- why London is sinking (isostatic adjustment)
- why sea levels (including in the Thames estuary) are rising
- the impact of climate change
- the appearance of landscapes across much of the northern hemisphere where a significant proportion of the land has been shaped in one way or another by glacial advances and retreats.

In these contexts, which show the potential significance of the topic, I would be prepared to argue that it is because glaciation is 'nothing to do with their lives' that it *deserves* a place in the (geography) school curriculum. The use of this anecdotal example is really to illustrate the significance of curriculum making. It is the discipline-based curriculum thinking that underpins the practical art of curriculum making that enables me to make the appropriate connections – and to be able to assert the 'relevance' of glaciation as a topic. I doubt that this kind of curriculum thinking is readily found among non-specialists. Indeed many specialist geographers may initially struggle to make appropriate and productive connections (if they themselves have not ever 'done' glaciations, for example – which is quite possible). These conclusions certainly have interesting implications for teacher education and training not least in terms of understanding curriculum thinking and what is meant by 'subject knowledge' development.

In this chapter we have explored the knowledge-led curriculum from the point of view of the teacher. The curriculum is perhaps one of the very few genuine educational ideas even though in many schools it often appears to be understood simplistically, as a management device and reduced in meaning to the timetable. It is a central concept in the knowledge-led school, and of great importance to teachers as it is concerned with the question of what to teach. In subjects in schools today, this question has never been more important, nor more difficult to answer. There are two main reasons why this is so. First, is the context of the 'knowledge society' in which information about the world is easily and very rapidly available, often for 'free'. The risk here is that information is confused with knowledge and that an illusion is created that teaching can be replaced with learning to learn. We have argued that this seriously risks dulling our ability to think for and beyond ourselves.

Secondly, and connected, is the inexorable rise of forms of 'pupil centredness' in which pupils' experience or 'voice' is deemed of paramount importance in influencing what should be taught. Effective curriculum making ensures that this is acknowledged and valued, but kept in its place. For equally important is the responsibility for teachers to take students beyond what they already know, or even think they want to know. In geography, pupils learn about a range of physical and human features and processes that shape and change the earth and its environments. They are often, rightly, asked to use this knowledge to interpret events in the news and also in their own lives. This is in line with constructivist theories of learning. This is good but not if it inadvertently fosters the idea that students must 'create' knowledge and can *only* discover meaning for themselves. As the quotation earlier indicates, this can easily place a limit on what teachers imagine they can (or should) teach children.

8

Future 3: Some implications, questions and concluding thoughts

David Lambert, Michael Young,
Carolyn Roberts and Martin Roberts

In deciding to write this book our major purpose was to intervene in, contribute to and hopefully influence current debates about the curriculum in England. It is a novel intervention in a number of ways. First, it was written by an unlikely combination of a teacher educator, a sociologist who has specialized in curriculum theory, a current headteacher and former headteacher, now Adviser. Secondly, it is a self-conscious effort on the part of the editors, who are more used to writing for their academic peers, to write for a broad readership. This readership includes heads (and their governors, and we hope, some parents) and teachers in schools as well as those who we normally think will be our readers – education faculty, teacher educators and students on postgraduate courses of various kinds.

This has encouraged us to try and write about what are often seen as the difficult 'knowledge' questions in as open and accessible style as possible. Insofar as we have been successful in achieving this, we have our two collaborating authors, Martin Roberts and Carolyn Roberts to thank and the many discussions we have had with them. It is they who convinced us that ideas which might have remained merely part of academic debates had a relevance to the day-to-day work of heads and their staff. In particular, they convinced us from their own experience that creating a successful school is not achieved by focusing solely, or even mainly, on the measurable outcomes of excellent teaching such as an 'outstanding' from Ofsted or the number of students getting particular grades at GCSE and A Level. This does not mean that these indices of success are not important for a school or for individual pupils and their parents. What Carolyn and Martin have stressed, as they express very clearly in their Preface, is the need for heads and their governors to look behind the data at the purposes of the school and how far they are expressed in the school's curriculum and the pedagogy of their teachers. If the whole staff are clear about and committed to their part in what a school is trying to do, improvement as measured by outcomes, will surely follow, even if measured success, for schools in different circumstances and with different histories, will not be the same.

That is why our message to heads is that first and foremost, they are curriculum leaders. They need to convince their staff that the school's curriculum defines its purposes and expresses the entitlement of all young people to the challenge and excitement of new knowledge. Success is about getting a grade 'A' or an 'A*', and for some a 'C' when they had feared it might be a 'D' or an 'E': but a school's *first* priority is that their students are excited about what they have learned and are left wanting to learn more. Everything else follows, as Carolyn Roberts remarks in her chapter. However, we acknowledge that it takes a degree of professional confidence, and often of past experience of 'success' to accept this in practice, for many of the current pressures on schools stress short-term performance. There are many international reports saying schools must instil in their pupils the familiar 'twenty-first-century skills' such as teamwork, communication and negotiation, and learning to learn. But what students could possibly find 'teamwork' exciting unless it was to do something that really mattered to them? Such 'generic' skills are beloved by policy makers and all too often by employers' representatives, but they can remain essentially vacuous in the context of a classroom, laboratory or studio that is not serving clear curriculum goals. Moreover, as expressions of the goals of schools, they can undermine their unique purpose. It is discovering something new that is exciting and whether it is another novel, why we can learn so much from an equation like $E = MC2$, Picasso's Guernica or some extraordinary historical event, and it is such knowledge that students can gain access to at school. To put it another way, if young people are not exposed to such knowledge, or for 'good educational reasons' are denied access to it, they will be deprived of their potential as free members of society. And why would we want to do that?

We thus take great exception to Dr Andreas Schleicher, the Deputy Director for Education and Skills at the OECD, when he pronounces that 'The past was about delivered wisdom, the future is about user-generated wisdom . . . the past was curriculum-centred, the future is learner-centred.' These are weasel words or worse: 'user-generated wisdom' – what could it possibly mean? And how could the future be learner-centred (other than in terms of the self-evident, obvious truth that human beings are, in Pearson PLC's current banal strap line, 'Always Learning'). The tragic thing is that these weasel words, which can so easily undermine teachers, are pronounced time and again with great authority. However, they are invariably stated by those who have gained higher degrees which they would never have achieved through a learner-centred curriculum. We doubt whether Schleicher himself would have had such a successful career if his school had relied on 'user-generated wisdom'! If all learning is already locked inside learners' heads, how does anyone learn anything or even need to?

One of the things that we hope this book will do is to give teachers confidence to know that schools are always involved in 'passing on' the knowledge acquired by earlier generations – new knowledge is always based on old knowledge and there are important things to learn from the past. Yes, schools were knowledge-centred in what we referred to as a Future 1 way and it is important that schools retain aspects in their approach to the curriculum that even future one-ists would recognize. Acquiring new knowledge, and getting the excitement that it brings is no less hard work than it ever was. However, what has changed is that whereas in a Future 1 curriculum it was 'knowledge for the few' (in which some pupils, mostly those in grammar and public schools, acquired much the same knowledge as their parents), today it must be 'knowledge for all'; furthermore, it is knowledge which builds on what their parents knew and takes them far beyond it.

In the remaining sections of this chapter, we want to touch on some of the more practical implications of our arguments, and help stimulate some debate and dialogue. We cannot offer a blueprint or some kind of 'roadmap' to what Future 3 schools will be like; even an attempt to do this would undermine part of our argument. For Future 3 as an idea, and its relationship to Futures 1 and 2 should be a debate that offers not a blueprint but a new way of thinking about the curriculum. This is not an exercise in 'deliverology'. It is much more about engaging with our readers, and schools (i.e. headteachers and their staff) taking back responsibility for the curriculum. Thus, we focus largely on human resource dimensions: governance, leadership and professional development. We leave a host of more technical issues, including assessment and information and communications technology, for example, to another volume.

The governance of schools and Future 3

One of the largest groups of volunteers in the United Kingdom is school governors: there are 300,000 governors who support 30,000 schools. Governing bodies have a range of duties and powers and a general responsibility for the conduct of the school with a view to promoting high standards of educational achievement. Their responsibilities include but are not limited to:

- setting targets for pupil achievement

- managing the school's finances

- making sure the curriculum is balanced and broadly based

- appointing staff

- reviewing staff performance and pay.

Four of those responsibilities may be measured and monitored if not easily, then at least with a degree of objectivity. The fifth, appropriately placed in the centre of the list, is harder for the typical governor to grasp. What is a 'balanced and broadly based curriculum'? Is it much the same as the 'rich and relevant' curriculum alluded to in the pages of the current Ofsted *Handbook* (2013)? Who is to judge?

Curriculum governance in a Future 1 school is easy – schools teach what they have always taught. Future 2 schools teach what they think will give young people skills for the future that they hope will be relevant to their current lives. Future 3 is inevitably harder: so what principles may governors call upon for guidance? The Learning and Achievement or Curriculum and Standards Committee of a Governing Body will take into account targets, to be sure, and receive reports from skilled or struggling staff, and be aware of Ofsted's most recent pronouncement on the state of the school. But how might governors seek to understand and choose from competing curriculum demands? How might governors recognize whether a particular curriculum model could restrict children's future opportunities? How might they recognize a market-driven solution which seeks to respond only to short-term preferences of children or parents, but not to the judgement of teachers? It is the head's curriculum priorities that usually become the governors', so what is her or his vision for the school? And if it comes to it, how might they argue with the head? A governor's closest relationship is with the head. Almost everything he or she knows about the school is filtered through the head. Even parent governors do not necessarily see the broad sweep of a school's work, and may have little knowledge of the local or national context.

How then can governors make decisions on what is right, broad and balanced (rich and relevant) in the curriculum?

Ofsted's *former* requirement of a Curriculum Statement required schools to declare their curriculum principles. A review or development of such a statement is a useful exercise for governors seeking to understand curriculum imperatives. They might begin by asking the following questions:

1 How do we describe the curriculum at this school?

2 Why is it organized this way?

3 Does this curriculum leave as many doors open to students as possible? And if so, how?

4 Is this curriculum designed to give the students a broad and balanced experience, or is it primarily geared to improving results for the performance tables? And are these two sets of goals in any way compatible?

5 What importance is given to teachers' own subject knowledge, when recruiting new staff?

6 Are students of all abilities given the opportunity to learn from teachers with high levels of subject knowledge?

Future 3 is based upon clear principles. A Future 3 school gives *all* children access to powerful knowledge. It combines this commitment with an approach to pedagogy that progressively extends access to the full range of curriculum subjects and convinces students and their parents that acquiring this knowledge is worthwhile and is their right.

Future 3 and the continuing professional development (CPD) of teachers

Before the introduction of the National Curriculum in 1991, much of the CPD on offer to teachers in England was subject based. Major providers were the specialist subject associations, LEA teachers' centres and university faculties of education. Before Kenneth Baker introduced the annual five compulsory INSET days in 1988, schools rarely organized their own CPD. Teachers chose which courses they wished to attend and the funding of them was the joint responsibility of schools, LEAs and the government. In the 1980s a limited number of teachers received the funding to undertake part-time masters degrees. Some local authorities even supported the secondment of teachers on full-time diploma and masters courses.

This was certainly no 'golden age' of CPD (or INSET as it was frequently called). Its quality varied enormously and the availability of good CPD opportunities was a bit like a postcode lottery. There was concern at the time about how investing in teachers' professional development on such an individualized basis impacted on the improvement of teaching and the educational outcomes of young people. This was linked to the emergence of 'whole curriculum' thinking, one outcome of which was to encourage teachers to shake off the perceived constraints of subject 'silos'.

It is therefore no surprise that as governments have increased their direct control of education since 1991 the overall amount of CPD has risen but the proportion of it which is subject centred and leading to a higher degree has greatly decreased. In 2004 the

NUT published a survey of CPD by MacBeath and Galton *A Life in Secondary Education: Finding Time for Learning*. They reported that 'subject based development opportunities were being severely curtailed. . . . On average teachers were spending three days a year on training for national initiatives, with one day a year allocated to all other initiatives.'

Schools have been encouraged to define professionalism as having an annual cycle of planning based on a school development plan which would lead to generic school improvement through performance management. It was these priorities that came to influence most opportunities for CPD under a setting we characterize as Futures 2 – largely generic, and learning (as opposed to knowledge) centred. Ofsted has reinforced this model of a 'new professionalism' with school-based CPD at its heart. In a 2006, Ofsted published a report *The Logical Chain: Continuing Professional Development in Effective Schools*. It concluded that 'the best results occurred when CPD was central to the schools improvement planning. Schools which integrated performance management, school review and development and CPD into a coherent cycle of planning improved the quality of teaching and raised standards.'

However, Leaton Gray and Denley (2005) do not share that essentially rosy view. In *The New Professionalism: A View from the Quagmire*, they argued that

Control is exercised over teachers' professional practice through managerialist approaches which emphasise performance over professional responsibility and autonomy. Despite the rhetoric, the reality of the 'new professionalism' reinforces the culture of low trust . . . teachers are being de-professionalised through challenges to their professional autonomy and lack of emphasis on their personal development needs, particularly in a subject-teaching context in favour of generic, institutionally-determined professional needs.

Leaton Gray (2006) has developed this view further and argued that subject-based professional development has become reduced to delivering key information relevant to specific examination specifications and/or government objectives and priorities. In effect, prevailing government priorities became the school's priorities, and teachers' professional responsibility – particularly in relation to what was being taught – was eroded.

Thus, the opportunities for subject-based CPD, perhaps with the exception of the STEM subjects, are small. Most CPD is school based, focusing on generic school improvement, especially improving exam results and impressing Ofsted. There is much to commend locating CPD in schools. However, one almost insurmountable problem with it is how to provide high-quality subject-focused professional development from within the school or even within a consortium of local schools, for almost by definition it needs to be led by subject specialists from outside the schools. What remained (until recently) were subject-oriented training meetings offered by examining groups, albeit oriented around 'improving results' reinforced by worksheets and lesson plans. Many retired headteachers occupy themselves with 'how to do well in an Ofsted inspection' consultancies. Headteachers, particularly of 'constrained' schools, are reluctant to release teachers for any CPD that is not related to examinations or Ofsted.

The Future 3 knowledge-led argument of this book points to a new and different approach. We cannot return to Future 1 and its association with the pre-1991 laissez faire approach to CPD. But equally, we cannot be satisfied with the current results oriented and essentially technicist school-based approach. It is also quite difficult to envisage schools, or even chains of schools or federations leading subject specialist CPD entirely from their own resources. Furthermore, a knowledge-led subject-based approach to CPD, as pioneered by some of the subject associations and the Prince's Teaching Institute is unlikely to be funded directly by government. Two changes are needed. First, a greatly expanded notion of accountability that is geared to the curriculum policies and priorities of individual schools, and secondly an approach to curriculum leadership of the kind we have advocated in this book which sees CPD as an instrument for achieving a school's curriculum goals as well as enhancing teachers' professionalism. In other words, we urge a move away from performance-led CPD towards a curriculum (and knowledge-led) CPD. This will be crucial if the knowledge-led approach to the curriculum that we advocate in this book is not to lead, as some will undoubtedly claim, to more students failing and thus to new inequalities.

Similar conclusions apply to those involved in initial teacher training. University-based PGCE courses tend not to be immediately sympathetic to the 'new professionalism' we described earlier (and which we link to a Future 2 scenario). However, the importance of subject knowledge in teaching – and in the practical application of curriculum thinking – has been undermined. Beginning teachers are certainly required to demonstrate their 'possession' of a secure specialist subject knowledge, but this is often determined through beginning-of-course 'subject knowledge audits'. We do not believe this represents the strongest of grounds to resist the instrumentalism and performance focus of successive waves of reform in initial teacher education. Indeed, we might say 'subject knowledge audits' belong to a Future 1 mindset. A Future 3 orientation of initial teacher preparation is urgently required, one that immerses beginning teachers in knowledge-led curriculum thinking from the start. This would require steady deliberation on the manner in which the subject to be taught really does provide access to powerful knowledge for *all* young people.

So what is to be done?

A bigger role for subject associations is a vital part of Future 3. It is difficult to generalize about these organizations as they have different histories, different constitutions and indeed different capacities (although they have all suffered contractions in recent years). However, they all have a significant role in linking subject teachers in schools with the developments in the related disciplines. They can lead debates and promote pedagogic development and innovation in their respective specialist fields. They can do this and provide opportunities for communicating new ideas through websites, journals and conferences. Most importantly, they are organizations which depend on the specialist professional knowledge of their members, with autonomy from both commercial and political interests.

However, as in any profession, the professional development of teachers requires resources, and they have to be found largely if not entirely by the members of the profession itself. At present these costs are largely covered by individual teachers or from their department budgets. Some schools carry the cost of annual subscriptions; more could be encouraged to do so as a symbol of the value a school places on teachers' specialist subject identities. The subject associations themselves – perhaps on the basis of expanding memberships – need to extend their brief as partners in the broader role of curriculum leadership that we are arguing for in this book. In broadening their role to fill the space created by the abolition of the Qualifications and Curriculum Development Authority (QCDA), subject associations could be one of the building blocks of the projected Royal College of Teaching.

Ofsted, the National College for Teaching and Leadership and Future 3

Achieving the kind of curriculum leadership in schools that we have argued for will, of course involve changes in the priorities of both Ofsted and the new National College for Teaching and Leadership. Both at present place more emphasis on performance than curriculum purposes. There is not the space to here to discuss the implications of schools adopting a Future 3 approach to the curriculum for either Ofsted or the National College. However at the very least it would involve both giving a greater emphasis to curriculum leadership.

As we have indicated, there are even more important implications of the idea of knowledge-led schools for initial teacher education. This is a large topic which requires an analysis of the constant changes in teacher training policies as well as an exploration of the implications of our three Futures approach to the curriculum. This again is beyond the scope of this short book, but there is much work to be done. However we intend to come back to the question in a follow-up volume, provisionally titled *Knowledge and the Future School (Volume 2): Subject Specialist Teachers and Knowledge Led Schools.*

Some questions and an invitation to a dialogue

The arguments presented in this book are quite complicated. They may be unsettling. Therefore, in this final section we have identified some questions that may strike readers arising from our Future 3 approach to the curriculum. We have faced many of them in conferences and some can be found in the educational literature.

QUESTION 1
Do Futures 1, 2 and 3 represent a linear, developmental sequence?

No.
The three-phase model was conceived in sequential terms but the implications of this were not explored in the original papers. Future 2 is best seen as a response to the rigidities and elitism of Future 1. However, Future 2 developed its own flaws which perpetuated inequalities in new ways. More recently, its 'anything goes' view of knowledge has been called into question and in particular its consequences for curricula designed for slow

learning pupils; this led to calls for a return to a new version of Future 1 as represented by the recent government reforms. We argue that both Futures 1 and 2 are inadequate as bases for a fairer and modern curriculum, albeit in different ways. To move beyond the limitations of Futures 1 and 2, we introduce the idea of Future 3. However, Future 3 is not as a new curriculum; it is a new way of thinking about the curriculum based on the entitlement to powerful knowledge for *all* pupils. Our starting point for Future 3, that it is a new way of thinking about the curriculum, quite distinct from Futures 1 and 2, is quite clear. However, what it involves more precisely needs exploration and development for it is possible that inspiring subject teaching in the past may have displayed many aspects of what we describe as Future 3. But with its emphasis on subjects and being knowledge-led and not learner-led, we are aware that Future 3 can easily be seen as little more than a return to Future 1.

QUESTION 2

Are Futures 1 and 2 equally bad?

No.

Some pupils will always acquire knowledge from a Future 1 curriculum; its major limitation was that it assumed knowledge was something to be 'complied with' rather than 'engaged with'. It is not surprising that it was a 'curriculum for the few'. The bigger villain for us is Future 2 as it rejects the idea of pupils 'acquiring knowledge' altogether. Future 2 teachers have lost confidence that there is 'better knowledge' that *all* pupils' are entitled to in *all* schools. However, rejecting Future 2 does not mean an inevitable return to the narrow 'givenness' and compliance of Future 1 that is epitomized by E. D. Hirsch's lists of what children 'need to know'.

QUESTION 3

Many of the children at my school are not academic: does this mean Future 3 does not apply to them?

No.

But it may mean that your curriculum is still trapped in Future 1.

Future 2 solutions such as skill-based and many prevocational programmes at 14+ (the RSA's Opening Minds is a good example) may appeal as 'quick fixes' for some children who appear to reject a subject-based curriculum. But for us this is more like a betrayal of those pupils. 'Academic' and 'Non-academic' may classify pupils with different levels of performance, attitude and motivation as fixed types. However, such a classification says little about a pupil's potential and can all too easily become a self-fulfilling prophesy. To think in these terms provides a shadow that hangs over education that is every bit as debilitating as the IQ. This is not to deny that however good a school's teachers are and however much effort they have put into creating an exciting curriculum, some pupils will make little effort and show little interest. This is a reality for all schools except those that are highly selective. What we are arguing is that a school has broadly two options. One is to develop a curriculum that combines an awareness of the community the school is located in with a clear sense of knowledge entitlement for all pupils. This maybe expressed in 100 per cent academic subject-based curriculum or some pathways that are not tied to academic subjects. The important issue in the latter case is that the non-academic pathways include access to the knowledge base of those pathways – this may be STEM, social science or humanities knowledge in an applied context. Thus students on such pathways will not be precluded from progression to higher level courses. Some of these students will of course remain uninterested, or may be disadvantaged or impeded in some way, and might not progress; at least, however, they have not been denied the opportunity. The more familiar alternative is that the focus of non-academic pathways is skill or competence based. As a consequence, students may gain a certificate at Levels 1 or 2 but they will have almost no chance to progress.

QUESTION 4

Do your criticisms of Future 2 mean the end of the 'teacher as a facilitator' and the return of the 'sage on the stage'?

No.

Of course teachers facilitate pupil learning. However, 'pedagogic adventures' in the form of 'learning activities' of one kind or another are not enough. Questionable claims that teachers should encourage and 'facilitate' discussion can easily slip into 'there are no right or wrong answers' and excessive moral relativism. It is a teacher's responsibility to make sure that pupils understand how to judge what 'the best' answers are to particular questions. It is teachers' concern for their subject knowledge that helps avoid such traps. Good teaching will always involve some lectures; and why not?

QUESTION 5

Isn't Future 3 simply Gradgrind in disguise?

No.

Future 3 is, it is worth repeating, a way of thinking about the curriculum that although no knowledge is fixed, there is 'better knowledge' in every field which pupils have a right of access to. It is about making arguments, giving reasons and where appropriate, providing evidence, rather than accumulating disconnected 'facts'. Influential figures like the OECD's Andreas Schleicher misunderstand what knowledge is and how it is acquired. He wants critical thinking, but you do not generate this through crudely simulating 'workplaces' or making schools look like open plan offices. Young people learn to be critical thinkers by engaging with concepts in different subject domains in which knowledge has been hard won, disputed and often is, unlike common sense, counter-intuitive. Some commentators would go even further and dispute whether a 'skills curriculum' can make any contribution at all the future of mankind on the planet: a 'curriculum of survival' must surely be knowledge led.

QUESTION 6

How does your knowledge-led curriculum lead to greater social justice and less inequality?

Here is something written by an American science educator:

The reason that anti-scientific sentiments have grave implications for education is that in modern societies there is not actually any alternative to science as a way of . . . [addressing] the endless flow of why and how questions that occur in any modern elementary school classroom where they are allowed to flourish. There is no alternative to biology that explains what bruises are, how you resemble your aunt more than you do your mother, why mosquitoes do not transmit AIDS, and why your nose runs when you have a cold.. . . For questions like these, the only real alternative to scientific inquiry is the suppression of inquiry; it is not some alternative form of knowing. (Cobern and Loving, 2008: 425–47)

The argument is not so straightforward in non-science subjects. However, it does remind us that we live in a world in which there is 'better knowledge' in all fields and that access to must be the starting point of a more just education system and less inequality. If there is no 'better knowledge' student progress becomes little more than personal opinion and in the worst cases 'giving teacher what he (or she) wants'. This does not mean that following a knowledge-led curriculum will guarantee that all pupils are successful; the distribution of success and failure in schools is not the responsibility of schools and their teachers alone. What a knowledge-led curriculum does for a school is to guarantee that *all* pupils and not just some, are *entitled* to knowledge. Furthermore, a knowledge-led school will hesitate to encourage slower learners to take 'easy' courses that may appear to suit them. This does not mean that schools do not offer subjects like Health and Social Care or Leisure and Tourism which have traditionally been assumed to be 'easier' to post-16 students. What it means is that a school with a knowledge-led curriculum will, before offering such courses, assess whether they as well as more 'traditional' subjects, give pupils access to powerful knowledge.

QUESTION 7

Is Future 3 *all* about teaching? What about learning: don't you just ignore what we know about children learning?

No.

At some stage, arising almost from nowhere, it became de rigeur to emphasize learning rather than teaching. In a way this became the code to denote that you were completely sold on the limitations of a Future 1 approach to the curriculum. We agree without question that good teachers are sensitive to how their students learn. Our problem is that a concern for learning has become an end in itself. This is illustrated by some overenthusiastic and sometimes ludicrous concerns for 'learning styles', and the overly bureaucratic implementation of 'assessment for learning' techniques. What we are against is what Gert Biesta describes memorably as 'learnification': the translation of everything there is to say about education in terms of learning and learners.

QUESTION 8

We have consistently improved the results profile of this school for several years now. Are you saying this is the wrong emphasis?

No.

Of course results matter. But just as the intensely competitive banking sector led up the 2008 collapse, we know that in education, 'results' are not enough. Results are important and a crucial measure of the 'effectiveness' of a school. But in themselves they measure little else – not even, as Ofsted inspectors have remarked, the quality of the subject teaching experienced by students.

Furthermore, what happens when the inexorable improvement of results falters – as it surely will? How does a school communicate its success and purpose then? It is in this scenario that confident and principled – and distributed – curriculum leadership is essential.

And by this we stress the knowledge centredness of this leadership, as the unique quality of any successful school community.

QUESTION 9

Your book goes on about the curriculum of a school but aren't schools largely driven by assessment and examinations, and it is 'teaching to the test' rather than the curriculum which shapes what a school can do?

Yes, unfortunately.

Of course we cannot but agree about the ever increasing pressures that examinations place on schools. The role of assessment is an enormous and in parts highly technical topic which is beyond the scope of this book, although Martin Roberts touched on some of the issues in Chapter 5. We are not against assessment or even external examinations; they are an inescapable and necessary part of all educational systems. Furthermore, teaching is no different from most service professions – teachers want to know whether their students are progressing in their understanding and use all kinds of informal means of checking this – questions in class, short tests, grading written assignments – all of which contribute to what we now know as formative assessment; it is part of the professional pedagogic role of teachers. The more this professional role of teachers is trusted, as with any other profession, the less important will be the other role of assessment, to inform public accountability. In an ideal world teachers would report their ranking of pupils on a common scale and that would be the basis of their being held accountable.

However, a brief comment can be made on the issue of assessment in light of our 'three futures' argument. The Future 1 system of assessment maintained high standards by 'selecting out' the majority, most of whom had left school before the examinations took place. It relied on a normative-referenced system that assumed a relatively fixed distribution of abilities and performance which changed little from year to year. The more flexible Future 2 approach to knowledge together with the vast expansion of candidates at 16+ and 18+ led to the opening up of types of assessment on the basis of a criterion reference rather than a normative reference system. This placed no formal limits on the proportion of candidates obtaining a particular grade. Thus pass rates and the proportion achieving higher grades increased from year to year. The expansion of numbers of candidates led to a vast and increasingly expensive and unwieldy system. At the same time growing doubts developed about whether the increased numbers of candidates with higher grades represented a real improvement of standards. As in its curriculum reforms, the current government is attempting to reverse the opening up of assessment by cutting back on continuous, modular and other locally based approaches to assessment in the hope that this will mean that higher grades and more passes will better represent increases in standards. To us this is to return to assumptions that held sway in the days of Future 1. What might a Future 3 approach to assessment and examinations involve? This, as with other complex areas like initial teacher education, has to be an issue we explore at a future date.

POSTSCRIPT – especially for headteachers

It is another week you are still worried by next year's predicted grades and spooked by horror stories of Ofsted's near and far. On top of that the Secretary of State has announced another mid-year change to accountability measures. Your heads of English and Maths are simultaneously confused, despondent, furious and stoical, but they will pick it all up tomorrow.

Yet you are not downhearted. You know what you stand for and what sort of education you provide for the young people clumsily thronging your corridors. You know that learning only happens when they have to think hard and work hard, and you are convinced that despite adolescent truculence they like it better that way. You have worked with teachers and governors alike on the idea of powerful knowledge this year, and even persuaded the arch-sceptics of the senior team to start thinking about the curriculum in terms of the 'three futures'. You are glad to be thinking clearly again. You know your curriculum principles can weather any storm.

Most of all, you know that your cause is just and that it will give disadvantaged young people a better chance to prosper in an unequal society. On good days, you think it will actually help to make society fairer. You close down your computer and, despite everything, permit yourself a quietly optimistic whistle as you head home.

APPENDIX 1

Further readings and references

Further readings

In this book, we have consciously adopted a personal and direct style, keeping academic references to a minimum. For readers who want to explore the theoretical basis of the ideas on which this book discusses, we suggest the following:

Moore, R. (2011) *Towards the Sociology of Truth*, Continuum Books, London.
Muller, J. (2000) *Reclaiming Knowledge*, Falmer/Routledge, London.
Rata, E. (2012) *The Politics of Knowledge in Education*, Routledge, Abingdon.
Sutherland, R. (2013) *Education and Social Justice in a Digital Age*, Policy
    Press, Bristol.
Wheelahan, L. (2009) *Why Knowledge Matters in Curriculum: A Social Realist
    Argument*, Routledge, Abingdon.
Young, M. (2008) *Bringing Knowledge Back In*, Routledge, London.

See also Michael Young's biographical essay in Edmund C. Short and Leonard J. Waks (eds) (2009) *Leaders in Curriculum Studies*, Sense Books, Rotterdam.

For those wanting to refer to Michael Young's earlier work, see his *Knowledge and Control*, Collier Macmillan, London. And for an incisive criticism of these and related ideas, we recommend Rob Moore and Johan Muller's 1999 article 'The Discourse of "Voice" and the Problem of Knowledge and Identity in the Sociology of Education', *British Journal of Sociology of Education*, 20, 2: 189–206.

For readers who are interested in how the ideas about knowledge and the
curriculum that we discuss in this book have been applied to specific school
subjects, we recommend the following from the Routledge series *Teaching
School Subjects 11–19*:

Davies, P. and Brant, J. (2005) *Business, Economics and Enterprise*
Kind, V. and Taber, K. (2005) *Science*
Morgan, J. and Lambert, D. (2005) *Geography*
Morgan, C., Watson, A. and Tikly, C. (2004) *Mathematics*
Pachler, N., Evans, M. and Lawes, S. (2007) *Modern Foreign Languages*

Details can be found at:
www.routledge.com/books/series/se0793

Subject Associations publish handbooks and teaching guides which are
usually strongly oriented to the knowledge specialism. In geography, for
example,
Roberts, M. (2013) *Geography through Enquiry*, Geographical Association,
    Sheffield.

Journals that include articles relevant to the discussions in this book are:

- *Journal of Curriculum Studies*
- *The Curriculum Journal*
- *British Journal of Sociology of Education*
- *International Studies in Sociology of Education*
- *European Journal of Education*
- *Journal of Education and Work*

A number of relevant reports and papers are in the public domain which are
also of relevance to the ideas developed in this book. For example,
Oates, T. (2010) *Could Do Better: Using International Comparisons to Refine
    the National Curriculum in England*, Cambridge Assessment. www.
    cambridgeassessment.org.uk/images/112281-could-do-better-using-
    international-comparisons-to-refine-the-national-curriculum-in-
    england.pdf
Institute of Ideas (2012) *Towards a Subject-Based Curriculum: A Policy
    Response from the IoI's Education Forum*. www.instituteofideas.com/
    events/educationforum.html

Either David Lambert or Michael Young would be happy to answer more
specific queries or comments from readers by email: m.young@ioe.ac.uk or
david.lambert@ioe.ac.uk.

References

Bernstein, B. (2000) *Pedagogy, Symbolic Control and Identity*, Oxford: Rowman and Littlefield.

Cobern, W. W. and Loving, C. C. (2008) An Essay for Educators: Epistemological Realism Really Is Common Sense, *Science and Education*, 17: 425–47.

Connell, R. (2012) Just Education, *Journal of Education Policy*, 27, 5: 681–3.

Cresswell, T. (2013) *Geographical Thought: A Critical Introduction*, London: Wiley-Blackwell.

DfE (2011) *The Framework for the National Curriculum*. A report by the expert panel for the national curriculum review, Crown Copyright (www.gov.uk/ government/uploads/system/uploads/attachment_data/file/175439/NCR-Expert_Panel_Report.pdf).

DfEE (1999) *Introducing the Revised National Curriculum*, London: DfEE/QCA.

Education Act 2002 (2002) www.legislation.gov.uk/ukpga/2002/32/contents

Firth, R. (2011) Making Geography Visible as an Object of Study in the Secondary School Curriculum, *Curriculum Journal*, 22, 3: 289–316.

GA (2009) *A Different View: A Manifesto from the Geographical Association*, Sheffield: Geographical Association.

Heppell, S. (2006) Once We Are 'Outside the Box' Will We Still Need It? in *21st Century Learning Environments*, OECD publishing (www.oecd.org).

Hirsch, E. D. (1987) *Cultural Literacy: What Every American Needs to Know*, Boston: Houghton Mifflin.

—. (2007) *The Knowledge Deficit*, Boston: Houghton Mifflin.

Hirst, P. (1974) *Knowledge and the Curriculum*, Abingdon: Routledge.

Lambert, D. and Hopkin, J. (2014) A Possibilist Analysis of the Geography National Curriculum in England, *International Research in Geographical and Environmental Education*, 23, 1: 64–78.

Leat, D. (1997) *Thinking through Geography*, Cambridge: Chris Kington Press.

Leaton Gray, S. (2006) *Teachers under Siege* Stoke-on-Trent: Trentham Books.

Leaton Gray, S. and Denley, P. (2005) *The 'New Professionalism' – Rhetoric and Realty? A View from the Quagmire*, a paper presented at the British Educational Research Association Conference, University of Glamorgan, September.

Le Grand, J. (2003) *Motivation, Agency and Public Policy*, Oxford: Oxford University Press.

Mansell, W. (2007) *Education by Number: The Tyranny of Testing*, London: Politico Press.

Marquand, D. (2004) *The Decline of the Public: The Hollowing Out of Citizenship*, Cambridge: Polity Press.

Moore, A. (ed.) (2006) *Schooling, Society and the Curriculum*, Abingdon: Routledge.

Naish, M. (1997) The Scope of School Geography: A Medium for Education. In D. Tilbury and M. Williams (eds), *Teaching and Learning Geography*, London: Routledge.

Oates, T. (2010) *Could Do Better: Using International Comparisons to Refine the National Curriculum in England*, Cambridge: Cambridge Assessment.

Peters, R. S. (1963) *Education as Initiation*, Inaugural Lecture (9 December 1963), London: Institute of Education.

Phenix, P. H. (1964) *Realms of Meaning*, New York: McGraw-Hill.

Pring, R. (2013) *The Life and Death of Secondary Education for All*. Abingdon: Routledge.

Rawding, C. (2013) How Does Geography Adapt to Changing Times? In D. Lambert and M. Jones (eds), *Debates in Geography Education*, London: Routledge.

Roberts, M. (2003) *Learning through Enquiry*, Sheffield: Geographical Association.

—. (2013) *Geography through Enquiry*, Sheffield: Geographical Association.

Schulman, L. (1986) Those Who Understand: Knowledge Growth in Teaching, *Educational Researcher*, 15, 2: 4–14.

Slater, F. (1983) *Learning through Enquiry: An Introduction to Activity Planning*, London: Heinemann.

Tomlinson, S. (2001) *Education in a Post-Welfare Society*, Buckingham: Open University Press.

Waters, M. (2013) *Thinking Allowed: On Schooling*, Camarthen: Independent Thinking Press.

White, J. (ed.) (2004) *Rethinking the School Curriculum*, London: RoutledgeFalmer.

Wolf, A. (2003) *Does Education Matter? Myths about Education and Economic Growth*, London: Penguin.

—. (2011) *The Wolf Report, Review of Vocational Education*, London: DfE/BIS (www.gov.uk/government/publications/review-of-vocational-education-the-wolf-report).

Young, M. F. D. (2008) *Bringing Knowledge Back In: From Social Constructivism to Social Realism in the Sociology of Education*, London: Routledge.

Young, M. F. D. and Muller, J. (2010) Three Educational Scenarios for the Future: Lessons from the Sociology of Knowledge, *European Journal of Education*, 45, 1: 11–27.

APPENDIX 2

The National Curriculum in England: A brief chronology

For readers who are not familiar with the development of the National Curriculum in England since 1988, we have included the following brief chronology.

1987   General Election Conservative victory.

1988   The Education Reform Act establishes the framework for the National Curriculum (NC). It was to be required of all publicly funded schools, but not of independent schools. The NC has four Key Stages: Key Stage 1, Years 1 and 2 (pupils aged 5 to 6); Key Stage 2, Years 3–6 (pupils aged 7 to 10); Key Stage 3, Years 7–9 (pupils aged 11–13); Key Stage 4, Years 10 and 11 (pupils aged 14 and 15). It is subject based with, initially, national testing at the end of each Key Stage. National testing for Key Stage 3 was abolished in 2008.

1989   NC introduced to primary schools and implemented across all key stages in the 1990s.

1991   National testing introduced.

1992   The Office for Standards in Education (Ofsted) introduced with the monitoring the NC and national test results a major responsibility.

1993   Review of the NC following teacher complaints that it was too unwieldy and complicated. Fewer subjects remained compulsory and the testing system was simplified.

1996   The NC complemented by the introduction of the National Literacy and Numeracy Strategies aimed mainly at primary schools.

1997   General Election Labour victory.

1999   National Curriculum Handbook expands and defines more clearly the aims of the NC.

2000   Curriculum framework extended to the early years (children from birth to 5).

2002   Citizenship added as an NC requirement.

2007   Another review reduces the specified content of the NC in secondary schools and encourages both greater flexibility and learning skills.

2010   General Election Coalition (mainly Conservative) government.

2011   Review of the NC which aims for greater rigour and more subject knowledge in the NC.

2013   Revised programmes of study published for consultation.

2014   Proposed date for the implementation of the revised NC, no longer required for academies and free schools though these are publicly funded.

Martin Roberts and David Lambert

INDEX

Page number in **bold** refers to figure.